Textbook Outlines, Highlights, and Practice Quizzes

Introducing Physical Geography

by Alan H. Strahler, 6th Edition

All "Just the Facts101" Material Written or Prepared by Cram101 Textbook Reviews

Title Page

"Just the Facts101" is a Content Technologies publication and tool designed to give you all the facts from your textbooks. Register for the full practice test for each of your chapters for virtually any of your textbooks.

Facts101 has built custom study tools specific to your textbook. We provide all of the factual testable information and unlike traditional study guides, we will never send you back to your textbook for more information.

YOU WILL NEVER HAVE TO HIGHLIGHT A BOOK AGAIN!

Facts101 StudyGuides
All of the information in this StudyGuide is written specifically for your textbook. We include the key terms, places, people, and concepts... the information you can expect on your next exam!

Facts101
Only Facts101 gives you the outlines, highlights, and PRACTICE TESTS specific to your textbook. Facts101 sister Cram101.com is an online application where you'll discover study tools designed to make the most of your limited study time.

www.Cram101.com

ISBN(s): 9781538832844. PUBX-8.20161219

STUDYING MADE EASY

This Craml0l notebook is designed to make studying easier and increase your comprehension of the textbook material. Instead of starting with a blank notebook and trying to write down everything discussed in class lectures, you can use this Craml0l textbook notebook and annotate your notes along with the lecture.

Our goal is to give you the best tools for success.

For a supreme understanding of the course, pair your notebook with our online tools at www.cram101.com

Our Online Access program is a simple way for us to keep our promise and provide you the best studying tools, regardless of where you purchased your Craml0l textbook notebook. As long as you let us know you are intereested in a free online access account we will set it up for you for 180 days.

Online Access:

SIMPLE STEPS TO GET A FREE ACCOUNT:

Email Travis.Reese@cram101.com

Include:

Order number

ISBN of Guide

Retailer where purchased

Introducing Physical Geography
Alan H. Strahler, 6th

CONTENTS

1. Physical Geography and the Tools Geographers Use

CHAPTER OUTLINE: KEY TERMS, PEOPLE, PLACES, CONCEPTS

- Weathering
- Antarctica
- Victoria Land
- Cape
- Cartography
- Climatology
- Physical geography
- Biogeography
- Ecological succession
- Geography
- Biosphere
- Lithosphere
- Carbon cycle
- Climate change
- Peninsula
- Global change
- Scale
- Greenhouse effect
- Geographic information system
- Global Positioning System
- Map projection

1. Physical Geography and the Tools Geographers Use

CHAPTER OUTLINE: KEY TERMS, PEOPLE, PLACES, CONCEPTS

Remote sensing

Statistic

SPRING

Maps

Meridian

Planar projection

Conformal map

Thematic map

Topographic map

Graphic scale

Choropleth map

National Park

Positioning system

Data acquisition

Electromagnetic radiation

Thermal radiation

Ice Sheet

Island

Lidar

Suspended load

Wind

1. Physical Geography and the Tools Geographers Use

CHAPTER OUTLINE: KEY TERMS, PEOPLE, PLACES, CONCEPTS

	Google Earth

CHAPTER HIGHLIGHTS & NOTES: KEY TERMS, PEOPLE, PLACES, CONCEPTS

Weathering	Weathering is the breaking down of rocks, soil and minerals as well as artificial materials through contact with the Earth's atmosphere, biota and waters. Weathering occurs in situ, roughly translated to: 'with no movement', and thus should not be confused with erosion, which involves the movement of rocks and minerals by agents such as water, ice, snow, wind, waves and gravity and then being transported and deposited in other locations. Two important classifications of weathering processes exist - physical and chemical weathering; each sometimes involves a biological component.
Antarctica	Antarctica is Earth's southernmost continent, containing the geographic South Pole. It is situated in the Antarctic region of the Southern Hemisphere, almost entirely south of the Antarctic Circle, and is surrounded by the Southern Ocean. At 14.0 million km^2 (5.4 million sq mi), it is the fifth-largest continent in area after Asia, Africa, North America, and South America. For comparison, Antarctica is nearly twice the size of Australia.
Victoria Land	Victoria Land is a region of Antarctica bounded on the east by the Ross Ice Shelf and the Ross Sea and on the west by Oates Land and Wilkes Land. It was discovered by Captain James Clark Ross in January 1841 and named after the UK's Queen Victoria. The rocky promontory of Minna Bluff is often regarded as the southernmost point of Victoria Land, and separates the Scott Coast to the north from the Hillary Coast of the Ross Dependency to the south.
Cape	In geography, a cape is a headland or promontory of large size extending into a body of water, usually the sea. A cape usually represents a marked change in trend of the coastline. Their proximity to the coastline makes them prone to natural forms of erosion, mainly tidal actions.
Cartography	Cartography is the study and practice of making maps. Combining science, aesthetics, and technique, cartography builds on the premise that reality can be modeled in ways that communicate spatial information effectively. The fundamental problems of traditional cartography are to:•Set the map's agenda and select traits of the object to be mapped.

1. Physical Geography and the Tools Geographers Use

CHAPTER HIGHLIGHTS & NOTES: KEY TERMS, PEOPLE, PLACES, CONCEPTS

Climatology	Climatology is the study of climate, scientifically defined as weather conditions averaged over a period of time. This modern field of study is regarded as a branch of the atmospheric sciences and a subfield of physical geography, which is one of the Earth sciences. Climatology now includes aspects of oceanography and biogeochemistry.
Physical geography	Physical geography is one of the two major sub-fields of geography. Physical geography is that branch of natural science which deals with the study of processes and patterns in the natural environment like the atmosphere, hydrosphere, biosphere, and geosphere, as opposed to the cultural or built environment, the domain of human geography. Within the body of physical geography, the Earth is often split either into several spheres or environments, the main spheres being the atmosphere, biosphere, cryosphere, geosphere, hydrosphere, lithosphere and pedosphere.
Biogeography	Biogeography is the study of the distribution of species and ecosystems in geographic space and through geological time. Organisms and biological communities vary in a highly regular fashion along geographic gradients of latitude, elevation, isolation and habitat area. Knowledge of spatial variation in the numbers and types of organisms is as vital to us today as it was to our early human ancestors, as we adapt to heterogeneous but geographically predictable environments.
Ecological succession	Ecological succession is the observed process of change in the species structure of an ecological community over time. The time scale can be decades (for example, after a wildfire), or even millions of years after a mass extinction. The community begins with relatively few pioneering plants and animals and develops through increasing complexity until it becomes stable or self-perpetuating as a climax community.
Geography	The Geography is Ptolemy's main work besides the Almagest. It is a treatise on cartography and a compilation of what was known about the world's geography in the Roman Empire of the 2nd century. Ptolemy relied mainly on the work of an earlier geographer, Marinos of Tyre, and on gazetteers of the Roman and ancient Persian empire.
Biosphere	The biosphere is the global sum of all ecosystems. It can also be termed as the zone of life on Earth, a closed system (apart from solar and cosmic radiation and heat from the interior of the Earth), and largely self-regulating. By the most general biophysiological definition, the biosphere is the global ecological system integrating all living beings and their relationships, including their interaction with the elements of the lithosphere, geosphere, hydrosphere, and atmosphere.
Lithosphere	The lithosphere is the rigid outermost shell of a rocky planet defined on the basis of the mechanical properties.

On Earth, it comprises the crust and the portion of the upper mantle that behaves elastically on time scales of thousands of years or greater. The outermost shell of a rocky planet defined on the basis of the chemistry and mineralogy is a crust.

Carbon cycle

The carbon cycle is the biogeochemical cycle by which carbon is exchanged among the biosphere, pedosphere, geosphere, hydrosphere, and atmosphere of the Earth. Along with the nitrogen cycle and the water cycle, the carbon cycle comprises a sequence of events that are key to making the Earth capable of sustaining life; it describes the movement of carbon as it is recycled and reused throughout the biosphere.

The global carbon budget is the balance of the exchanges (incomes and losses) of carbon between the carbon reservoirs or between one specific loop (e.g., atmosphere ? biosphere) of the carbon cycle.

Climate change

Climate change is a significant and lasting change in the statistical distribution of weather patterns over periods ranging from decades to millions of years. It may be a change in average weather conditions, or in the distribution of weather around the average conditions (i.e., more or fewer extreme weather events). Climate change is caused by factors such as biotic processes, variations in solar radiation received by Earth, plate tectonics, and volcanic eruptions.

Peninsula

A peninsula is a piece of land that is bordered by water on three sides but connected to mainland. The surrounding water is usually understood to belong to a single, contiguous body, but is not always explicitly defined as such. In many Germanic and Celtic languages and also in Baltic, Slavic, Hungarian, Chinese, Hebrew and Korean, peninsulas are called 'half-islands'.

Global change

Global change refers to planetary-scale changes in the Earth system. The system consists of the land, oceans, atmosphere, poles, life, the planet's natural cycles and deep Earth processes. These constituent parts influence one another.

Scale

The scale of a map is the ratio of a distance on the map to the corresponding distance on the ground. This simple concept is complicated by the curvature of the Earth's surface, which forces scale to vary across a map. Because of this variation, the concept of scale becomes meaningful in two distinct ways.

Greenhouse effect

The greenhouse effect is a process by which thermal radiation from a planetary surface is absorbed by atmospheric greenhouse gases, and is re-radiated in all directions. Since part of this re-radiation is back towards the surface and the lower atmosphere, it results in an elevation of the average surface temperature above what it would be in the absence of the gases.

1. Physical Geography and the Tools Geographers Use

CHAPTER HIGHLIGHTS & NOTES: KEY TERMS, PEOPLE, PLACES, CONCEPTS

Geographic information system

A geographic information system is a system designed to capture, store, manipulate, analyze, manage, and present all types of geographical data. The acronym Geographic information system is sometimes used for geographical information science or geospatial information studies to refer to the academic discipline or career of working with geographic information systems and is a large domain within the broader academic discipline of Geoinformatics.

A Geographic information system can be thought of as a system that provides spatial data entry, management, retrieval, analysis, and visualization functions.

Global Positioning System

The Global Positioning System is a space-based satellite navigation system that provides location and time information in all weather conditions, anywhere on or near the Earth where there is an unobstructed line of sight to four or more Global Positioning System satellites. The system provides critical capabilities to military, civil and commercial users around the world. It is maintained by the United States government and is freely accessible to anyone with a Global Positioning System receiver.

Map projection

A map projection is a systematic transformation of the latitudes and longitudes of locations on the surface of a sphere or an ellipsoid into locations on a plane. Map projections are necessary for creating maps. All map projections distort the surface in some fashion.

Remote sensing

Remote sensing is the acquisition of information about an object or phenomenon without making physical contact with the object. In modern usage, the term generally refers to the use of aerial sensor technologies to detect and classify objects on Earth (both on the surface, and in the atmosphere and oceans) by means of propagated signals (e.g. electromagnetic radiation). It may be split into active remote sensing, when a signal is first emitted from aircraft or satellites) or passive (e.g. sunlight) when information is merely recorded.

Statistic

A statistic is a single measure of some attribute of a sample (e.g., its arithmetic mean value). It is calculated by applying a function (statistical algorithm) to the values of the items of the sample, which are known together as a set of data.

More formally, statistical theory defines a statistic as a function of a sample where the function itself is independent of the sample's distribution; that is, the function can be stated before realization of the data.

SPRING

SPRING is a freeware GIS and remote sensing image processing system with an object-oriented data model which provides for the integration of raster and vector data representations in a single environment. It has Windows and Linux versions and provides a comprehensive set of functions, including tools for Satellite Image Processing, Digital Terrain Modeling, Spatial Analysis, Geostatistics, Spatial Statistics, Spatial Databases and Map Management.

Maps

Maps is a mapping service application developed by Apple Inc. for its iOS and OS X operating systems. It allows turn-by-turn navigation by car or walk including re-routing.

Meridian

A meridian is the great circle passing through the celestial poles and the zenith of a particular location. Consequently, it also contains the horizon's north and south points and it is perpendicular to the celestial equator and the celestial horizon. This celestial meridian matches the projection, onto the celestial sphere, of the terrestrial meridian.

Planar projection

Planar projections are the subset of 3D graphical projections constructed by linearly mapping points in three-dimensional space to points on a two-dimensional projection plane. The projected point on the plane is chosen such that it is collinear with the corresponding three-dimensional point and the centre of projection. The lines connecting these points are commonly referred to as projectors.

Conformal map

In mathematics, a conformal map is a function which preserves angles. In the most common case the function has a domain and range in the complex plane.

More formally, a map, $f : U \rightarrow V$ with $U, V \subset \mathbb{R}^n$

is called conformal (or angle-preserving) at a point u_0 if it preserves oriented angles between curves through u_0 with respect to their orientation (i.e., not just the magnitude of the angle).

Thematic map

A thematic map is a type of map or chart especially designed to show a particular theme connected with a specific geographic area. These maps 'can portray physical, social, political, cultural, economic, sociological, agricultural, or any other aspects of a city, state, region, nation, or continent'.

Topographic map

In modern mapping, a topographic map is a type of map characterized by large-scale detail and quantitative representation of relief, usually using contour lines but, historically, using a variety of methods. Traditional definitions require a topographic map to show both natural and man-made features. A topographic map is typically published as a map series, made up of two or more map sheets that combine to form the whole map.

Graphic scale

A linear scale, also called a bar scale, scale bar, graphic scale, or graphical scale, is a means of visually showing the scale of a map, nautical chart, engineering drawing, or architectural drawing.

On large scale maps and charts, those covering a small area, and engineering and architectural drawings, the linear scale can be very simple, a line marked at intervals to show the distance on the earth or object which the distance on the scale represents. A person using the map can use a pair of dividers (or, less precisely, two fingers) to measure a distance by comparing it to the linear scale.

1. Physical Geography and the Tools Geographers Use

CHAPTER HIGHLIGHTS & NOTES: KEY TERMS, PEOPLE, PLACES, CONCEPTS

Choropleth map

A choropleth map, ('area/region' + 'multitude') is a thematic map in which areas are shaded or patterned in proportion to the measurement of the statistical variable being displayed on the map, such as population density or per-capita income.

The choropleth map provides an easy way to visualize how a measurement varies across a geographic area or it shows the level of variability within a region.

A special type of choropleth map is a prism map, a three-dimensional map in which a given region's height on the map is proportional to the statistical variable's value for that region.

National Park

A national park is a park in use for conservation purposes. Often it is a reserve of natural, semi-natural, or developed land that a sovereign state declares or owns. Although individual nations designate their own national parks differently, there is a common idea: the conservation of 'wild nature' for posterity and as a symbol of national pride.

Positioning system

A positioning system is a mechanism for determining the location of an object in space. Technologies for this task exist ranging from worldwide coverage with meter accuracy to workspace coverage with sub-millimetre accuracy.

Data acquisition

Data acquisition is the process of sampling signals that measure real world physical conditions and converting the resulting samples into digital numeric values that can be manipulated by a computer. Data acquisition systems, abbreviated by the acronyms DAS or DAQ, typically convert analog waveforms into digital values for processing. The components of data acquisition systems include:•Sensors, to convert physical parameters to electrical signals.•Signal conditioning circuitry, to convert sensor signals into a form that can be converted to digital values.•Analog-to-digital converters, to convert conditioned sensor signals to digital values.

Data acquisition applications are usually controlled by software programs developed using various general purpose programming languages such as Assembly, BASIC, C, C++, C#, Fortran, Java, LabVIEW, Lisp, Pascal, etc.

Electromagnetic radiation

Electromagnetic radiation is the radiant energy released by certain electromagnetic processes. Visible light is one type of electromagnetic radiation; other familiar forms are invisible to the human eye, such as radio waves, infrared light and X-rays.

Classically, electromagnetic radiation consists of electromagnetic waves, which are synchronized oscillations of electric and magnetic fields that propagate at the speed of light through a vacuum.

Thermal radiation

Thermal radiation is electromagnetic radiation generated by the thermal motion of charged particles in matter. All matter with a temperature greater than absolute zero emits thermal radiation.

Ice Sheet

An ice sheet is a mass of glacier ice that covers surrounding terrain and is greater than 50,000 km^2, thus also known as continental glacier. The only current ice sheets are in Antarctica and Greenland; during the last glacial period at Last Glacial Maximum (LGM) the Laurentide ice sheet covered much of North America, the Weichselian ice sheet covered northern Europe and the Patagonian Ice Sheet covered southern South America.

Ice sheets are bigger than ice shelves or alpine glaciers. Masses of ice covering less than 50,000 km^2 are termed an ice cap.

Island

An island or isle is any piece of sub-continental land that is surrounded by water. Very small islands such as emergent land features on atolls can be called islets, skerries, cays or keys. An island in a river or a lake island may be called an eyot or ait, or a holm.

Lidar

Lidar is a remote sensing technology that measures distance by illuminating a target with a laser and analyzing the reflected light. Although erroneously considered to be an acronym of LIght Detection And Ranging, the term lidar was actually created as a portmanteau of 'light' and 'radar.'

Lidar is popularly used as a technology used to make high resolution maps, with applications in geomatics, archaeology, geography, geology, geomorphology, seismology, forestry, remote sensing, atmospheric physics, airborne laser swath mapping (ALSM), laser altimetry, and contour mapping.

Suspended load

Suspended load is the portion of the sediment that is carried by a fluid flow which settle slowly enough such that it almost never touches the bed. It is maintained in suspension by the turbulence in the flowing water and consists of particles generally of the fine sand, silt and clay size.

Wind

Wind is the flow of gases on a large scale. On the surface of the Earth, wind consists of the bulk movement of air. In outer space, solar wind is the movement of gases or charged particles from the sun through space, while planetary wind is the outgassing of light chemical elements from a planet's atmosphere into space.

Google Earth

Google Earth is a virtual globe, map and geographical information program that was originally called EarthViewer 3D created by Keyhole, Inc, a Central Intelligence Agency funded company acquired by Google in 2004 . It maps the Earth by the superimposition of images obtained from satellite imagery, aerial photography and geographic information system (GIS) 3D globe. It was available under three different licenses, two now: Google Earth, a free version with limited function; Google Earth Plus (discontinued), which included additional features; and Google Earth Pro ($399 per year), which is intended for commercial use.

1. Physical Geography and the Tools Geographers Use

CHAPTER QUIZ: KEY TERMS, PEOPLE, PLACES, CONCEPTS

1. _________ refers to planetary-scale changes in the Earth system. The system consists of the land, oceans, atmosphere, poles, life, the planet's natural cycles and deep Earth processes. These constituent parts influence one another.

   a. CLARREO
   b. Global change
   c. Climate change
   d. Climate change and gender

2. The _________ is the rigid outermost shell of a rocky planet defined on the basis of the mechanical properties. On Earth, it comprises the crust and the portion of the upper mantle that behaves elastically on time scales of thousands of years or greater. The outermost shell of a rocky planet defined on the basis of the chemistry and mineralogy is a crust.

   a. Lithosphere
   b. Bridge scour
   c. British Society for Geomorphology
   d. Catena

3. _________ is a region of Antarctica bounded on the east by the Ross Ice Shelf and the Ross Sea and on the west by Oates Land and Wilkes Land. It was discovered by Captain James Clark Ross in January 1841 and named after the UK's Queen Victoria. The rocky promontory of Minna Bluff is often regarded as the southernmost point of _________, and separates the Scott Coast to the north from the Hillary Coast of the Ross Dependency to the south.

   a. Victoria Land
   b. Herbert Range
   c. Mawson Station
   d. Mount Breckinridge

4. The _________ of a map is the ratio of a distance on the map to the corresponding distance on the ground. This simple concept is complicated by the curvature of the Earth's surface, which forces _________ to vary across a map. Because of this variation, the concept of _________ becomes meaningful in two distinct ways.

   a. Scale
   b. Biological anthropology
   c. Cartographic aggression
   d. Cartographic propaganda

5. . _________ is the radiant energy released by certain electromagnetic processes. Visible light is one type of _________; other familiar forms are invisible to the human eye, such as radio waves, infrared light and X-rays.

   Classically, _________ consists of electromagnetic waves, which are synchronized oscillations of electric and magnetic fields that propagate at the speed of light through a vacuum.

   a. Essay on the Principle of Population
   b. Cadastre

c. Catalan chart

d. Electromagnetic radiation

ANSWER KEY
1. Physical Geography and the Tools Geographers Use

---

1. b
2. a
3. a
4. a
5. d

---

2. The Earth as a Rotating Planet

CHAPTER OUTLINE: KEY TERMS, PEOPLE, PLACES, CONCEPTS

- Antarctica
- Geoid
- North Pole
- South Pole
- Equator
- Meridian
- Tide
- Great circle
- Latitude
- Longitude
- Prime meridian
- Elevation
- Ice Sheet
- Map projection
- Mercator projection
- Conformal map
- Winkel Tripel
- Winkel tripel projection
- Hydrology
- Iran
- Ice field

2. The Earth as a Rotating Planet

CHAPTER OUTLINE: KEY TERMS, PEOPLE, PLACES, CONCEPTS

- Atomic time
- Hydraulic action
- Suspended load
- Season
- September equinox
- Solstice
- Subsolar point
- Summer solstice
- Vernal equinox
- Winter solstice
- Antarctic Circle
- Arctic Circle
- Tropic of Capricorn
- Declination

2. The Earth as a Rotating Planet

CHAPTER HIGHLIGHTS & NOTES: KEY TERMS, PEOPLE, PLACES, CONCEPTS

Antarctica	Antarctica is Earth's southernmost continent, containing the geographic South Pole. It is situated in the Antarctic region of the Southern Hemisphere, almost entirely south of the Antarctic Circle, and is surrounded by the Southern Ocean. At 14.0 million km^2 (5.4 million sq mi), it is the fifth-largest continent in area after Asia, Africa, North America, and South America. For comparison, Antarctica is nearly twice the size of Australia.
Geoid	The geoid is the shape that the surface of the oceans would take under the influence of Earth's gravitation and rotation alone, in the absence of other influences such as winds and tides. All points on that surface have the same scalar potential--there is no difference in potential energy between any two. Specifically, the geoid is the equipotential surface that would coincide with the mean ocean surface of the Earth if the oceans and atmosphere were in equilibrium, at rest relative to the rotating Earth, and extended through the continents (such as with very narrow canals).
North Pole	The North Pole, also known as the Geographic North Pole or Terrestrial North Pole, is defined as the point in the Northern Hemisphere where the Earth's axis of rotation meets its surface. It should not be confused with the North Magnetic Pole. The North Pole is the northernmost point on the Earth, lying diametrically opposite the South Pole.
South Pole	The South Pole, also known as the Geographic South Pole or Terrestrial South Pole, is one of the two points where the Earth's axis of rotation intersects its surface. It is the southernmost point on the surface of the Earth and lies on the opposite side of the Earth from the North Pole. Situated on the continent of Antarctica, it is the site of the United States Amundsen-Scott South Pole Station, which was established in 1956 and has been permanently staffed since that year.
Equator	An equator is the intersection of a sphere's surface with the plane perpendicular to the sphere's axis of rotation and midway between the poles. The Equator usually refers to the Earth's equator: an imaginary line on the Earth's surface equidistant from the North Pole and South Pole, dividing the Earth into the Northern Hemisphere and Southern Hemisphere. Other planets and astronomical bodies have equators similarly defined.
Meridian	A meridian is the great circle passing through the celestial poles and the zenith of a particular location. Consequently, it also contains the horizon's north and south points and it is perpendicular to the celestial equator and the celestial horizon. This celestial meridian matches the projection, onto the celestial sphere, of the terrestrial meridian.
Tide	Tides are the rise and fall of sea levels caused by the combined effects of the gravitational forces exerted by the Moon and the Sun and the rotation of the Earth.

Some shorelines experience two almost equal high tides and two low tides each day, called a semi-diurnal tide. Some locations experience only one high and one low tide each day, called a diurnal tide.

Great circle

A great circle, also known as an orthodrome or Riemannian circle, of a sphere is the intersection of the sphere and a plane that passes through the center point of the sphere. This partial case of a circle of a sphere is opposed to a small circle, the intersection of the sphere and a plane that does not pass through the center. Any diameter of any great circle coincides with a diameter of the sphere, and therefore all great circles have the same circumference as each other, and have the same center as the sphere.

Latitude

In geography, latitude is a geographic coordinate that specifies the north-south position of a point on the Earth's surface. Latitude is an angle (defined below) which ranges from 0° at the Equator to 90° (North or South) at the poles. Lines of constant latitude, or parallels, run east-west as circles parallel to the equator.

Longitude

Longitude, is a geographic coordinate that specifies the east-west position of a point on the Earth's surface. It is an angular measurement, usually expressed in degrees and denoted by the Greek letter lambda (?). Points with the same longitude lie in lines running from the North Pole to the South Pole.

Prime meridian

A prime meridian is a meridian, i.e., a line of longitude, at which longitude is defined to be 0°. A prime meridian and its opposite in a 360°-system, the 180th meridian (at 180° longitude), form a great circle.

This great circle divides the sphere, e.g., the Earth, into two hemispheres.

Elevation

The elevation of a geographic location is its height above a fixed reference point, most commonly a reference geoid, a mathematical model of the Earth's sea level as an equipotential gravitational surface . Elevation, or geometric height, is mainly used when referring to points on the Earth's surface, while altitude or geopotential height is used for points above the surface, such as an aircraft in flight or a spacecraft in orbit, and depth is used for points below the surface.

Less commonly, elevation is measured using the center of the Earth as the reference point.

Ice Sheet

An ice sheet is a mass of glacier ice that covers surrounding terrain and is greater than 50,000 km^2, thus also known as continental glacier. The only current ice sheets are in Antarctica and Greenland; during the last glacial period at Last Glacial Maximum (LGM) the Laurentide ice sheet covered much of North America, the Weichselian ice sheet covered northern Europe and the Patagonian Ice Sheet covered southern South America.

Ice sheets are bigger than ice shelves or alpine glaciers. Masses of ice covering less than 50,000 km^2 are termed an ice cap.

Map projection

A map projection is a systematic transformation of the latitudes and longitudes of locations on the surface of a sphere or an ellipsoid into locations on a plane. Map projections are necessary for creating maps. All map projections distort the surface in some fashion.

Mercator projection

The Mercator projection is a cylindrical map projection presented by the Flemish geographer and cartographer Gerardus Mercator in 1569. It became the standard map projection for nautical purposes because of its ability to represent lines of constant course, known as rhumb lines or loxodromes, as straight segments which conserve the angles with the meridians. While the linear scale is equal in all directions around any point, thus preserving the angles and the shapes of small objects (which makes the projection conformal), the Mercator projection distorts the size and shape of large objects, as the scale increases from the Equator to the poles, where it becomes infinite.

Conformal map

In mathematics, a conformal map is a function which preserves angles. In the most common case the function has a domain and range in the complex plane.

More formally, a map, $f : U \rightarrow V$ with $U, V \subset \mathbb{R}^n$

is called conformal (or angle-preserving) at a point u_0 if it preserves oriented angles between curves through u_0 with respect to their orientation (i.e., not just the magnitude of the angle).

Winkel Tripel

The Winkel tripel projection, a modified azimuthal map projection of the world, is one of three projections proposed by Oswald Winkel in 1921. The projection is the arithmetic mean of the equirectangular projection and the Aitoff projection: The name Tripel (German for 'triple') refers to Winkel's goal of minimizing three kinds of distortion: area, direction, and distance.

Winkel tripel projection

The Winkel tripel projection, a modified azimuthal map projection, is one of three projections proposed by Oswald Winkel in 1921. The projection is the arithmetic mean of the equirectangular projection and the Aitoff projection: The name Tripel (German for 'triple') refers to Winkel's goal of minimizing three kinds of distortion: area, direction and distance.

Hydrology

Hydrology is the study of the movement, distribution, and quality of water on Earth and other planets, including the hydrologic cycle, water resources and environmental watershed sustainability. A practitioner of hydrology is a hydrologist, working within the fields of earth or environmental science, physical geography, geology or civil and environmental engineering.

Hydrology is subdivided into surface hydrology and marine hydrology.

Iran

Iran, also known as Persia (or), officially the Islamic Republic of Iran, is a country in Western Asia.

	It is bordered to the northwest by Armenia and Azerbaijan, with Kazakhstan and Russia across the Caspian Sea; to the northeast by Turkmenistan; to the east by Afghanistan and Pakistan; to the south by the Persian Gulf and the Gulf of Oman; and to the west by Turkey and Iraq. Comprising a land area of 1,648,195 km^2 (636,372 sq mi), it is the second-largest nation in the Middle East and the 18th-largest in the world; with 78.4 million inhabitants, Iran is the world's 17th most populous nation.
Ice field	An ice field is an area less than 50,000 km^2 (19,000 sq mi) of ice often found in the colder climates and higher altitudes of the world where there is sufficient precipitation. It is an extensive area of interconnected valley glaciers from which the higher peaks rise as nunataks. Ice fields are larger than alpine glaciers, smaller than ice sheets and similar in area to ice caps.
Atomic time	International Atomic Time is a high-precision atomic coordinate time standard based on the notional passage of proper time on Earth's geoid. It is the basis for Coordinated Universal Time (UTC), which is used for civil timekeeping all over the Earth's surface, and for Terrestrial Time, which is used for astronomical calculations. As of 30 June 2015 when the last leap second was added, TAI is exactly 36 seconds ahead of UTC. The 36 seconds results from the initial difference of 10 seconds at the start of 1972, plus 26 leap seconds in UTC since 1972.
Hydraulic action	Hydraulic action is erosion that occurs when the motion of water against a rock surface produces mechanical weathering. Most generally, it is the ability of moving water (flowing or waves) to dislodge and transport rock particles. Within this rubric are a number of specific erosional processes, including abrasion, attrition, corrasion, saltation, and scouring.
Suspended load	Suspended load is the portion of the sediment that is carried by a fluid flow which settle slowly enough such that it almost never touches the bed. It is maintained in suspension by the turbulence in the flowing water and consists of particles generally of the fine sand, silt and clay size.
Season	A season is a subdivision of the year, marked by changes in weather, ecology, and hours of daylight. Seasons result from the yearly revolution of the Earth around the Sun and the tilt of the Earth's axis relative to the plane of revolution. In temperate and polar regions, the seasons are marked by changes in the intensity of sunlight that reaches the Earth's surface, variations of which may cause animals to go into hibernation or to migrate, and plants to be dormant.
September equinox	The September equinox is the moment when the Sun appears to cross the celestial equator, heading southward. Due to differences between the calendar year and the tropical year, the September equinox can occur at any time from the 21st to the 24th day of September. At the equinox, the Sun rises directly in the east and sets directly in the west.
Solstice	A solstice is an astronomical event that occurs twice each year as the Sun reaches its highest or lowest excursion relative to the celestial equator on the celestial sphere.

Both the solstices and the equinoxes are directly connected with the seasons of the year.

The term solstice can also be used in a broader sense, as the day when this occurs.

Subsolar point

The subsolar point on a planet is where its sun is perceived to be directly overhead, that is where the sun's rays are hitting the planet exactly perpendicular to its surface. It can also mean the point closest to the sun on an object in space, even though the sun might not be visible.

For planets with an orientation and rotation similar to the Earth's, the subsolar point will move westward, circling the globe once a day, but it will also move north and south between the tropics over the course of a year.

Summer solstice

The summer solstice occurs when the tilt of a planet's semi-axis, in either northern or southern hemispheres, is most inclined toward the star that it orbits. Earth's maximum axial tilt toward the Sun is 23° 26'. This happens twice each year (once in each hemisphere), at which times the Sun reaches its highest position in the sky as seen from the north or the south pole.

Vernal equinox

The March equinox or Northward equinox is the equinox on the Earth when the Sun appears to leave the southern hemisphere and cross the celestial equator, heading northward as seen from earth. In the Northern Hemisphere the March equinox is known as the vernal equinox, and in the Southern Hemisphere as the autumnal equinox.

On the Gregorian calendar the Northward equinox can occur as early as March 19 or as late as March 21. For a common year the computed time slippage is about 5 hours 49 minutes later than the previous year, and for a leap year about 18 hours 11 minutes earlier than the previous year.

Winter solstice

Winter solstice is an astronomical phenomenon marking the shortest day and the longest night of the year. In the Northern Hemisphere this is the December solstice and in the Southern Hemisphere this is the June solstice.

The axial tilt of Earth and gyroscopic effects of its daily rotation mean that the two opposite points in the sky to which the Earth's axis of rotation points (axial precession) change very slowly (making a complete circle approximately every 26,000 years).

Antarctic Circle

The Antarctic Circle is one of the five major circles of latitude that mark maps of the Earth. For 2012, it is the parallel of latitude that runs 66° 33' 44? (or 66.5622°) south of the Equator.

Arctic Circle

The Arctic Circle is one of the five major circles of latitude that mark maps of the Earth. In 2012, it is the parallel of latitude that runs 66° 33' 44? (or 66.5622°) north of the Equator.

2. The Earth as a Rotating Planet

CHAPTER HIGHLIGHTS & NOTES: KEY TERMS, PEOPLE, PLACES, CONCEPTS

Tropic of Capricorn	The Tropic of Capricorn is the circle of latitude that contains the subsolar point on the December (or southern) solstice. It is thus the southernmost latitude where the Sun can be directly overhead. Its northern equivalent is the Tropic of Cancer.
Declination	In astronomy, declination is one of the two angles that locate a point on the celestial sphere in the equatorial coordinate system, the other being hour angle. Declination's angle is measured north or south of the celestial equator, along the hour circle passing through the point in question. The root of word the declination means 'a bending away' or 'a bending down'.

CHAPTER QUIZ: KEY TERMS, PEOPLE, PLACES, CONCEPTS

1. The _________ on a planet is where its sun is perceived to be directly overhead, that is where the sun's rays are hitting the planet exactly perpendicular to its surface. It can also mean the point closest to the sun on an object in space, even though the sun might not be visible.

   For planets with an orientation and rotation similar to the Earth's, the _________ will move westward, circling the globe once a day, but it will also move north and south between the tropics over the course of a year.

   a. Celestial coordinate system
   b. Subsolar point
   c. Celestial pole
   d. Celestial sphere

2. A _________ is the great circle passing through the celestial poles and the zenith of a particular location. Consequently, it also contains the horizon's north and south points and it is perpendicular to the celestial equator and the celestial horizon. This celestial _________ matches the projection, onto the celestial sphere, of the terrestrial _________.

   a. Celestial coordinate system
   b. Meridian
   c. Celestial pole
   d. Celestial sphere

3. . _________ is an astronomical phenomenon marking the shortest day and the longest night of the year. In the Northern Hemisphere this is the December solstice and in the Southern Hemisphere this is the June solstice.

The axial tilt of Earth and gyroscopic effects of its daily rotation mean that the two opposite points in the sky to which the Earth's axis of rotation points (axial precession) change very slowly (making a complete circle approximately every 26,000 years).

a. Mughal Empire
b. Russian Empire
c. Survival International
d. Winter solstice

4. _________ is Earth's southernmost continent, containing the geographic South Pole. It is situated in the Antarctic region of the Southern Hemisphere, almost entirely south of the Antarctic Circle, and is surrounded by the Southern Ocean. At 14.0 million km^2 (5.4 million sq mi), it is the fifth-largest continent in area after Asia, Africa, North America, and South America. For comparison, _________ is nearly twice the size of Australia.

a. Antarctica
b. Land hemisphere
c. Australian Antarctic Territory
d. Abyssal plain

5. _________s are the rise and fall of sea levels caused by the combined effects of the gravitational forces exerted by the Moon and the Sun and the rotation of the Earth.

Some shorelines experience two almost equal high _________s and two low _________s each day, called a semi-diurnal _________. Some locations experience only one high and one low _________ each day, called a diurnal _________.

a. Benchmark
b. Bessel ellipsoid
c. Tide
d. Chronometric singularity

ANSWER KEY
2. The Earth as a Rotating Planet

---

1. b
2. b
3. d
4. a
5. c

---

3. The Earth`s Global Energy Balance

CHAPTER OUTLINE: KEY TERMS, PEOPLE, PLACES, CONCEPTS

- Ozone
- Ozone layer
- Electromagnetic radiation
- Middle East
- Shortwave radiation
- Spectrum
- Ultraviolet radiation
- Visible light
- Wavelength
- Solar constant
- Current
- Ocean current
- Absorption
- National Park
- Scattering
- Cloud
- Insolation
- Longwave
- Radiation
- Weathering
- Latitude

3. The Earth`s Global Energy Balance

CHAPTER OUTLINE: KEY TERMS, PEOPLE, PLACES, CONCEPTS

Equator

North Pole

Tropic of Capricorn

Arctic tundra

Strip mining

National Forest

Carbon dioxide

Greenhouse effect

Oxidation

Water vapor

Ice age

Latent Heat

Sensible heat

Atmosphere

Climate model

Thunderstorm

Erosion

Climograph

3. The Earth`s Global Energy Balance

CHAPTER HIGHLIGHTS & NOTES: KEY TERMS, PEOPLE, PLACES, CONCEPTS

Ozone	Ozone, or trioxygen, is an inorganic compound with the chemical formula O3(μ-O) (also written [O (μ-O)O] or O3). It is a pale blue gas with a distinctively pungent smell. It is an allotrope of oxygen that is much less stable than the diatomic allotrope O2, breaking down in the lower atmosphere to normal dioxygen.
Ozone layer	The ozone layer or ozone shield refers to a region of Earth's stratosphere that absorbs most of the Sun's ultraviolet radiation. It contains high concentrations of ozone (O_3) relative to other parts of the atmosphere, although still very small relative to other gases in the stratosphere. The ozone layer contains less than 10 parts per million of ozone, while the average ozone concentration in Earth's atmosphere as a whole is only about 0.3 parts per million.
Electromagnetic radiation	Electromagnetic radiation is the radiant energy released by certain electromagnetic processes. Visible light is one type of electromagnetic radiation; other familiar forms are invisible to the human eye, such as radio waves, infrared light and X-rays. Classically, electromagnetic radiation consists of electromagnetic waves, which are synchronized oscillations of electric and magnetic fields that propagate at the speed of light through a vacuum.
Middle East	The Middle East is a region that roughly encompasses a majority of Western Asia (excluding the Caucasus) and Egypt. The term is used as a synonym for Near East, in opposition to Far East. The corresponding adjective is Middle Eastern and the derived noun is Middle Easterner.
Shortwave radiation	Shortwave radiation is radiant energy with wavelengths in the visible (VIS), near-ultraviolet (UV), and near-infrared (NIR) spectra. There is no standard cut-off for the near-infrared range; therefore, the shortwave radiation range is also variously defined. It may be broadly defined to include all radiation with a wavelength between 0.1μm and 5.0μm or narrowly defined so as to include only radiation between 0.2μm and 3.0μm.
Spectrum	A spectrum is a condition that is not limited to a specific set of values but can vary infinitely within a continuum. The word was first used scientifically within the field of optics to describe the rainbow of colors in visible light when separated using a prism. As scientific understanding of light advanced, it came to apply to the entire electromagnetic spectrum.
Ultraviolet radiation	Ultraviolet light is an electromagnetic radiation with a wavelength from 10 nm (30 PHz) to 380 nm (750 THz), shorter than that of visible light but longer than X-rays. UV radiation is present in sunlight, and also produced by electric arcs and specialized lights such as mercury-vapor lamps, tanning lamps, and black lights. Although lacking the energy to ionize atoms, long-wavelength ultraviolet radiation can cause chemical reactions, and causes many substances to glow or fluoresce.
Visible light	Light is electromagnetic radiation within a certain portion of the electromagnetic spectrum.

The word usually refers to visible light, which is visible to the human eye and is responsible for the sense of sight. Visible light is usually defined as having wavelengths in the range of 400-700 nanometres (nm), or 4.00×10^{-7} to 7.00×10^{-7} m, between the infrared (with longer wavelengths) and the ultraviolet (with shorter wavelengths).

Wavelength

In physics, the wavelength of a sinusoidal wave is the spatial period of the wave--the distance over which the wave's shape repeats, and the inverse of the spatial frequency. It is usually determined by considering the distance between consecutive corresponding points of the same phase, such as crests, troughs, or zero crossings and is a characteristic of both traveling waves and standing waves, as well as other spatial wave patterns. Wavelength is commonly designated by the Greek letter lambda (?).

Solar constant

The solar constant, a measure of flux density, is the amount of incoming solar electromagnetic radiation per unit area that would be incident on a plane perpendicular to the rays, at a distance of one astronomical unit (AU) (roughly the mean distance from the Sun to the Earth). The solar constant includes all types of solar radiation, not just the visible light. It is measured by satellite to be roughly 1.361 kilowatts per square meter (kW/m^2) at solar minimum and approximately 0.1% greater (roughly 1.362 kW/m^2) at solar maximum.

Current

A current, in a river or stream, is the flow of water influenced by gravity as the water moves downhill to reduce its potential energy. The current varies spatially as well as temporally within the stream, dependent upon the flow volume of water, stream gradient, and channel geometrics. In tidal zones, the current in rivers and streams may reverse on the flood tide before resuming on the ebb tide.

Ocean current

An ocean current is a continuous, directed movement of seawater generated by the forces acting upon this mean flow, such as breaking waves, wind, Coriolis effect, cabbeling, temperature and salinity differences and tides caused by the gravitational pull of the Moon and the Sun. Depth contours, shoreline configurations and interaction with other currents influence a current's direction and strength. A deep current is any ocean current at a depth of greater than 100m.

Absorption

In physics, absorption of electromagnetic radiation is the way in which the energy of a photon is taken up by matter, typically the electrons of an atom. Thus, the electromagnetic energy is transformed into internal energy of the absorber, for example thermal energy. The reduction in intensity of a light wave propagating through a medium by absorption of a part of its photons is often called attenuation.

National Park

A national park is a park in use for conservation purposes. Often it is a reserve of natural, semi-natural, or developed land that a sovereign state declares or owns. Although individual nations designate their own national parks differently, there is a common idea: the conservation of 'wild nature' for posterity and as a symbol of national pride.

3. The Earth`s Global Energy Balance

CHAPTER HIGHLIGHTS & NOTES: KEY TERMS, PEOPLE, PLACES, CONCEPTS

Scattering

Scattering is a general physical process where some forms of radiation, such as light, sound, or moving particles, are forced to deviate from a straight trajectory by one or more paths due to localized non-uniformities in the medium through which they pass. In conventional use, this also includes deviation of reflected radiation from the angle predicted by the law of reflection. Reflections that undergo scattering are often called diffuse reflections and unscattered reflections are called specular (mirror-like) reflections.

Cloud

In meteorology, a cloud is a visible mass of liquid droplets or frozen crystals made of water or various chemicals suspended in the atmosphere above the surface of a planetary body. These suspended particles are also known as aerosols and are studied in the cloud physics branch of meteorology.

Terrestrial cloud formation is the result of air in Earth's atmosphere becoming saturated due to either or both of two processes; cooling of the air and adding water vapor.

Insolation

Insolation is a measure of solar radiation energy received on a given surface area and recorded during a given time. It is also called solar irradiation and expressed as 'hourly irradiation' if recorded during an hour or 'daily irradiation' if recorded during a day. The unit recommended by the World Meteorological Organization is megajoules per square metre (MJ/m^2) or joules per square millimetre (J/mm^2).

Longwave

In radio, longwave refers to parts of the radio spectrum with relatively long wavelengths. The term is a historic one dating from the early 20th century, when the radio spectrum was considered to consist of long, medium and short wavelengths. Most modern radio systems and devices use wavelengths which would then have been considered 'ultra-short'.

Radiation

In physics, radiation is the emission or transmission of energy in the form of waves or particles through space or through a material medium. This includes:•electromagnetic radiation, such as radio waves, visible light, x-rays, and gamma radiation•particle radiation, such as alpha radiation beta radiation and neutron radiation•acoustic radiation, such as ultrasound, sound, and seismic waves (dependent on a physical transmission medium)•gravitational radiation, radiation that takes the form of gravitational waves, or ripples in the curvature of spacetime.

Radiation is often categorized as either ionizing or non-ionizing depending on the energy of the radiated particles. Ionizing radiation carries more than 10 eV, which is enough to ionize atoms and molecules, and break chemical bonds.

Weathering

Weathering is the breaking down of rocks, soil and minerals as well as artificial materials through contact with the Earth's atmosphere, biota and waters. Weathering occurs in situ, roughly translated to: 'with no movement', and thus should not be confused with erosion, which involves the movement of rocks and minerals by agents such as water, ice, snow, wind, waves and gravity and then being transported and deposited in other locations.

Latitude	In geography, latitude is a geographic coordinate that specifies the north-south position of a point on the Earth's surface. Latitude is an angle (defined below) which ranges from 0° at the Equator to 90° (North or South) at the poles. Lines of constant latitude, or parallels, run east-west as circles parallel to the equator.
Equator	An equator is the intersection of a sphere's surface with the plane perpendicular to the sphere's axis of rotation and midway between the poles. The Equator usually refers to the Earth's equator: an imaginary line on the Earth's surface equidistant from the North Pole and South Pole, dividing the Earth into the Northern Hemisphere and Southern Hemisphere. Other planets and astronomical bodies have equators similarly defined.
North Pole	The North Pole, also known as the Geographic North Pole or Terrestrial North Pole, is defined as the point in the Northern Hemisphere where the Earth's axis of rotation meets its surface. It should not be confused with the North Magnetic Pole. The North Pole is the northernmost point on the Earth, lying diametrically opposite the South Pole.
Tropic of Capricorn	The Tropic of Capricorn is the circle of latitude that contains the subsolar point on the December (or southern) solstice. It is thus the southernmost latitude where the Sun can be directly overhead. Its northern equivalent is the Tropic of Cancer.
Arctic tundra	In physical geography, tundra is a type of biome where the tree growth is hindered by low temperatures and short growing seasons. The term tundra comes through Russian ?????? (tûndra) from the Kildin Sami word tundâr 'uplands', 'treeless mountain tract'. There are three types of tundra: arctic tundra, alpine tundra, and Antarctic tundra.
Strip mining	Surface mining, including strip mining, open-pit mining and mountaintop removal mining, is a broad category of mining in which soil and rock overlying the mineral deposit are removed. In contrast to underground mining, in which the overlying rock is left in place, and the mineral removed through shafts or tunnels. Surface mining began in the mid-sixteenth century and is practiced throughout the world, although the majority of surface mining occurs in North America. It gained popularity throughout the 20th century, and is now the predominant form of mining in coal beds such as those in Appalachia and America's Midwest.
National Forest	The National Forest is an environmental project in central England run by the National Forest Company. Portions of Leicestershire, Derbyshire and Staffordshire, 200 square miles (520 km^2) are being planted, in an attempt to blend ancient woodland with new plantings to create a new national forest. It stretches from the outskirts of Leicester in the east to Burton upon Trent in the west, and is planned link the ancient forests of Needwood and Charnwood.

3. The Earth`s Global Energy Balance

CHAPTER HIGHLIGHTS & NOTES: KEY TERMS, PEOPLE, PLACES, CONCEPTS

Carbon dioxide

Carbon dioxide is a naturally occurring chemical compound composed of two oxygen atoms each covalently double bonded to a single carbon atom. It is a gas at standard temperature and pressure and exists in Earth's atmosphere in this state, as a trace gas at a concentration of 0.039 per cent by volume.

As part of the carbon cycle, plants, algae, and cyanobacteria use light energy to photosynthesize carbohydrate from carbon dioxide and water, with oxygen produced as a waste product.

Greenhouse effect

The greenhouse effect is a process by which thermal radiation from a planetary surface is absorbed by atmospheric greenhouse gases, and is re-radiated in all directions. Since part of this re-radiation is back towards the surface and the lower atmosphere, it results in an elevation of the average surface temperature above what it would be in the absence of the gases.

Solar radiation at the frequencies of visible light largely passes through the atmosphere to warm the planetary surface, which then emits this energy at the lower frequencies of infrared thermal radiation.

Oxidation

Redox is a contraction of the name for a chemical reduction-oxidation reaction. A reduction reaction always occurs with an oxidation reaction. Redox reactions include all chemical reactions in which atoms have their oxidation state changed; in general, redox reactions involve the transfer of electrons between chemical species.

Water vapor

Water vapor, water vapour or aqueous vapor, is the gaseous phase of water. It is one state of water within the hydrosphere. Water vapor can be produced from the evaporation or boiling of [illegible] or from the sublimation of ice.

Ice age

[illegible] or more precisely, a glacial age, is a period of long-term reduction in the temperature of [illegible] surface and atmosphere, resulting in the presence or expansion of continental and [illegible] ets and alpine glaciers. Within a long-term ice age, individual pulses of cold climate [illegible] lacial periods' (or alternatively 'glacials' or 'glaciations' or colloquially as 'ice age'), and [illegible] arm periods are called 'interglacials'. Glaciologically, ice age implies the presence of [illegible] sheets in the northern and southern hemispheres.

Latent Heat

Latent heat is energy released or absorbed, by a body or a thermodynamic system, during a constant-temperature process that is specified in some way. An example is latent heat of fusion for a phase change, melting, at a specified temperature and pressure. The term was introduced around 1762 by Scottish chemist Joseph Black.

Sensible heat

Sensible heat is heat exchanged by a body or thermodynamic system that changes the temperature, and some macroscopic variables of the body, but leaves unchanged certain other macroscopic variables, such as volume or pressure.

Atmosphere

An atmosphere is a layer of gases surrounding a planet or other material body of sufficient mass that is held in place by the gravity of the body. An atmosphere is more likely to be retained if the gravity is high and the atmosphere's temperature is low.

The atmosphere of Earth, which is mostly nitrogen, also contains oxygen used by most organisms for respiration and carbon dioxide used by plants, algae and cyanobacteria for photosynthesis, also protects living organisms from genetic damage by solar ultraviolet radiation.

Climate model

Climate models use quantitative methods to simulate the interactions of the atmosphere, oceans, land surface, and ice. They are used for a variety of purposes from study of the dynamics of the climate system to projections of future climate. The most talked-about use of climate models in recent years has been to project temperature changes resulting from increases in atmospheric concentrations of greenhouse gases.

Thunderstorm

A thunderstorm, also known as an electrical storm, a lightning storm, thundershower or simply a storm, is a form of turbulent weather characterized by the presence of lightning and its acoustic effect on the Earth's atmosphere known as thunder. The meteorologically assigned cloud type associated with the thunderstorm is the cumulonimbus. Thunderstorms are usually accompanied by strong winds, heavy rain and sometimes snow, sleet, hail, or no precipitation at all.

Erosion

In earth science, erosion is the action of surface processes that remove soil, rock, or dissolved material from one location on the Earth's crust, then transport it away to another location. The particulate breakdown of rock or soil into clastic sediment is referred to as physical or mechanical erosion; this contrasts with chemical erosion, where soil or rock material is removed from an area by its dissolving into a solvent (typically water), followed by the flow away of that solution. Eroded sediment or solutes may be transported just a few millimetres, or for thousands of kilometres.

Climograph

A climograph is a graphical representation of basic climatic parameters, that is monthly average temperature and precipitation, at a certain location. It is used for a quick-view of the climate of a location.

3. The Earth`s Global Energy Balance

CHAPTER QUIZ: KEY TERMS, PEOPLE, PLACES, CONCEPTS

1. Surface mining, including _________, open-pit mining and mountaintop removal mining, is a broad category of mining in which soil and rock overlying the mineral deposit are removed. In contrast to underground mining, in which the overlying rock is left in place, and the mineral removed through shafts or tunnels.

   Surface mining began in the mid-sixteenth century and is practiced throughout the world, although the majority of surface mining occurs in North America. It gained popularity throughout the 20th century, and is now the predominant form of mining in coal beds such as those in Appalachia and America's Midwest.

   a. Mughal Empire
   b. 10th parallel south
   c. 11th parallel north
   d. Strip mining

2. _________ is heat exchanged by a body or thermodynamic system that changes the temperature, and some macroscopic variables of the body, but leaves unchanged certain other macroscopic variables, such as volume or pressure.

   a. Sensible heat
   b. Sensible heat
   c. Russian Empire
   d. Bramertonian Stage

3. _________ is the breaking down of rocks, soil and minerals as well as artificial materials through contact with the Earth's atmosphere, biota and waters. _________ occurs in situ, roughly translated to: 'with no movement', and thus should not be confused with erosion, which involves the movement of rocks and minerals by agents such as water, ice, snow, wind, waves and gravity and then being transported and deposited in other locations.

   Two important classifications of _________ processes exist - physical and chemical _________; each sometimes involves a biological component.

   a. Mughal Empire
   b. Direct insolation
   c. Weathering
   d. Teniente Luis Carvajal Villaroel Antarctic Base

4. _________, water vapour or aqueous vapor, is the gaseous phase of water. It is one state of water within the hydrosphere. _________ can be produced from the evaporation or boiling of liquid water or from the sublimation of ice.

   a. Mughal Empire
   b. Water vapor
   c. Climate change
   d. Climate change and gender

5. . _________, or trioxygen, is an inorganic compound with the chemical formula O3(μ-O) (also written [O(μ-O)O] or O3).

It is a pale blue gas with a distinctively pungent smell. It is an allotrope of oxygen that is much less stable than the diatomic allotrope O2, breaking down in the lower atmosphere to normal dioxygen.

a. Ozone
b. Bay mud
c. Bioconversion
d. Biogeochemistry

ANSWER KEY
3. The Earth`s Global Energy Balance

---

1. d
2. a
3. c
4. b
5. a

---

4. Air Temperature

CHAPTER OUTLINE: KEY TERMS, PEOPLE, PLACES, CONCEPTS

- Antarctica
- Island
- Greenhouse effect
- Biogeography
- Carbon dioxide
- Elevation
- Forest
- Latitude
- National Forest
- Current
- Geography
- Ocean current
- Climate change
- Latent Heat
- Solar constant
- Radiation
- Evapotranspiration
- Transpiration
- Urban heat
- Urban heat island
- Moraine

4. Air Temperature

CHAPTER OUTLINE: KEY TERMS, PEOPLE, PLACES, CONCEPTS

- Range
- Wind
- Temperature gradient
- Temperature inversion
- Heat index
- Alpine tundra
- Atlantic
- Lapse rate
- Troposphere
- Atmosphere
- Tundra
- Mesosphere
- Stratopause
- Insolation
- Subsidence
- Isothermal
- Siberia
- Temperature record
- Weather satellite
- Sea surface temperature
- Coral reef

4. Air Temperature

CHAPTER OUTLINE: KEY TERMS, PEOPLE, PLACES, CONCEPTS

- National Park
- Tree
- Coral
- Arctic
- Global warming
- Climate
- Lithosphere
- Sea-level rise
- Sea ice
- Ecosystem
- Habitat
- Kyoto Protocol
- Greenhouse gas

4. Air Temperature

CHAPTER HIGHLIGHTS & NOTES: KEY TERMS, PEOPLE, PLACES, CONCEPTS

Antarctica	Antarctica is Earth's southernmost continent, containing the geographic South Pole. It is situated in the Antarctic region of the Southern Hemisphere, almost entirely south of the Antarctic Circle, and is surrounded by the Southern Ocean. At 14.0 million km^2 (5.4 million sq mi), it is the fifth-largest continent in area after Asia, Africa, North America, and South America. For comparison, Antarctica is nearly twice the size of Australia.
Island	An island or isle is any piece of sub-continental land that is surrounded by water. Very small islands such as emergent land features on atolls can be called islets, skerries, cays or keys. An island in a river or a lake island may be called an eyot or ait, or a holm.
Greenhouse effect	The greenhouse effect is a process by which thermal radiation from a planetary surface is absorbed by atmospheric greenhouse gases, and is re-radiated in all directions. Since part of this re-radiation is back towards the surface and the lower atmosphere, it results in an elevation of the average surface temperature above what it would be in the absence of the gases. Solar radiation at the frequencies of visible light largely passes through the atmosphere to warm the planetary surface, which then emits this energy at the lower frequencies of infrared thermal radiation.
Biogeography	Biogeography is the study of the distribution of species and ecosystems in geographic space and through geological time. Organisms and biological communities vary in a highly regular fashion along geographic gradients of latitude, elevation, isolation and habitat area. Knowledge of spatial variation in the numbers and types of organisms is as vital to us today as it was to our early human ancestors, as we adapt to heterogeneous but geographically predictable environments.
Carbon dioxide	Carbon dioxide is a naturally occurring chemical compound composed of two oxygen atoms each covalently double bonded to a single carbon atom. It is a gas at standard temperature and pressure and exists in Earth's atmosphere in this state, as a trace gas at a concentration of 0.039 per cent by volume. As part of the carbon cycle, plants, algae, and cyanobacteria use light energy to photosynthesize carbohydrate from carbon dioxide and water, with oxygen produced as a waste product.
Elevation	The elevation of a geographic location is its height above a fixed reference point, most commonly a reference geoid, a mathematical model of the Earth's sea level as an equipotential gravitational surface . Elevation, or geometric height, is mainly used when referring to points on the Earth's surface, while altitude or geopotential height is used for points above the surface, such as an aircraft in flight or a spacecraft in orbit, and depth is used for points below the surface.

Forest	A forest, also referred to as a wood or the woods, is an area with a high density of trees. As with cities, depending on various cultural definitions, what is considered a forest may vary significantly in size and have different classifications according to how and of what the forest is composed. A forest is usually an area filled with trees but any tall densely packed area of vegetation may be considered a forest, even underwater vegetation such as kelp forests, or non-vegetation such as fungi, and bacteria.
Latitude	In geography, latitude is a geographic coordinate that specifies the north-south position of a point on the Earth's surface. Latitude is an angle (defined below) which ranges from 0° at the Equator to 90° (North or South) at the poles. Lines of constant latitude, or parallels, run east-west as circles parallel to the equator.
National Forest	The National Forest is an environmental project in central England run by the National Forest Company. Portions of Leicestershire, Derbyshire and Staffordshire, 200 square miles (520 km^2) are being planted, in an attempt to blend ancient woodland with new plantings to create a new national forest. It stretches from the outskirts of Leicester in the east to Burton upon Trent in the west, and is planned link the ancient forests of Needwood and Charnwood.
Current	A current, in a river or stream, is the flow of water influenced by gravity as the water moves downhill to reduce its potential energy. The current varies spatially as well as temporally within the stream, dependent upon the flow volume of water, stream gradient, and channel geometrics. In tidal zones, the current in rivers and streams may reverse on the flood tide before resuming on the ebb tide.
Geography	The Geography is Ptolemy's main work besides the Almagest. It is a treatise on cartography and a compilation of what was known about the world's geography in the Roman Empire of the 2nd century. Ptolemy relied mainly on the work of an earlier geographer, Marinos of Tyre, and on gazetteers of the Roman and ancient Persian empire.
Ocean current	An ocean current is a continuous, directed movement of seawater generated by the forces acting upon this mean flow, such as breaking waves, wind, Coriolis effect, cabbeling, temperature and salinity differences and tides caused by the gravitational pull of the Moon and the Sun. Depth contours, shoreline configurations and interaction with other currents influence a current's direction and strength. A deep current is any ocean current at a depth of greater than 100m.
Climate change	Climate change is a significant and lasting change in the statistical distribution of weather patterns over periods ranging from decades to millions of years. It may be a change in average weather conditions, or in the distribution of weather around the average conditions (i.e., more or fewer extreme weather events). Climate change is caused by factors such as biotic processes, variations in solar radiation received by Earth, plate tectonics, and volcanic eruptions.

4. Air Temperature

CHAPTER HIGHLIGHTS & NOTES: KEY TERMS, PEOPLE, PLACES, CONCEPTS

Latent Heat	Latent heat is energy released or absorbed, by a body or a thermodynamic system, during a constant-temperature process that is specified in some way. An example is latent heat of fusion for a phase change, melting, at a specified temperature and pressure. The term was introduced around 1762 by Scottish chemist Joseph Black.
Solar constant	The solar constant, a measure of flux density, is the amount of incoming solar electromagnetic radiation per unit area that would be incident on a plane perpendicular to the rays, at a distance of one astronomical unit (AU) (roughly the mean distance from the Sun to the Earth). The solar constant includes all types of solar radiation, not just the visible light. It is measured by satellite to be roughly 1.361 kilowatts per square meter (kW/m²) at solar minimum and approximately 0.1% greater (roughly 1.362 kW/m²) at solar maximum.
Radiation	In physics, radiation is the emission or transmission of energy in the form of waves or particles through space or through a material medium. This includes:•electromagnetic radiation, such as radio waves, visible light, x-rays, and gamma radiation•particle radiation, such as alpha radiation beta radiation and neutron radiation•acoustic radiation, such as ultrasound, sound, and seismic waves (dependent on a physical transmission medium)•gravitational radiation, radiation that takes the form of gravitational waves, or ripples in the curvature of spacetime. Radiation is often categorized as either ionizing or non-ionizing depending on the energy of the radiated particles. Ionizing radiation carries more than 10 eV, which is enough to ionize atoms and molecules, and break chemical bonds.
Evapotranspiration	Evapotranspiration is the sum of evaporation and plant transpiration from the Earth's land surface to atmosphere. Evaporation accounts for the movement of water to the air from sources such as the soil, canopy interception, and waterbodies. Transpiration accounts for the movement of water within a plant and the subsequent loss of water as vapor through stomata in its leaves.
Transpiration	Transpiration is the process of water movement through a plant and its evaporation from aerial parts, such as leaves, stems and flowers. Water is necessary for plants but only a small amount of water taken up by the roots is used for growth and metabolism. The remaining 97-99.5% is lost by transpiration and guttation.
Urban heat	An urban heat island is a city or metropolitan area that is significantly warmer than its surrounding rural areas due to human activities. The phenomenon was first investigated and described by Luke Howard in the 1810s, although he was not the one to name the phenomenon. The temperature difference usually is larger at night than during the day, and is most apparent when winds are weak.
Urban heat island	An urban heat island is a metropolitan area that is significantly warmer than its surrounding rural areas due to human activities. The phenomenon was first investigated and described by Luke Howard in the 1810s, although he was not the one to name the phenomenon.

Moraine	A moraine is any glacially formed accumulation of unconsolidated glacial debris that occurs in currently glaciated and formerly glaciated regions on Earth (i.e. a past glacial maximum), through geomorphological processes. Moraines are formed from debris previously carried along by a glacier and normally consist of somewhat rounded particles ranging in size from large boulders to minute glacial flour. Lateral moraines are formed at the side of the ice flow and terminal moraines at the foot, marking the maximum advance of the glacier.
Range	In biology, the range or distribution of a species is the geographical area within which that species can be found. Within that range, dispersion is variation in local density. The term is often qualified:•Sometimes a distinction is made between a species' native range and the places to which it has been introduced by human agency (deliberately or accidentally), as well as where it has been re-introduced following extirpation.•for species found in different regions at different times of year, terms such as summer range and winter range are often employed.•For species for which only part of their range is used for breeding activity, the terms breeding range and non-breeding range are not used.•For mobile animals, the term natural range is often used, as opposed to areas where it occurs as a vagrant.•Geographic or temporal qualifiers are often added: for example, British range or pre-1950 range. There are at least five types of distribution patterns:•Scattered/random (Random placement)•Clustered/grouped (Most are placed in one area)•Linear (Their placements form a line)•Radial (Placements form an ' x ' shape)•Regular/ordered (They are not random at all, but follow a set placement.
Wind	Wind is the flow of gases on a large scale. On the surface of the Earth, wind consists of the bulk movement of air. In outer space, solar wind is the movement of gases or charged particles from the sun through space, while planetary wind is the outgassing of light chemical elements from a planet's atmosphere into space.
Temperature gradient	A temperature gradient is a physical quantity that describes in which direction and at what rate the temperature changes the most rapidly around a particular location. The temperature gradient is a dimensional quantity expressed in units of degrees (on a particular temperature scale) per unit length. The SI unit is kelvin per meter (K/m).
Temperature inversion	In meteorology, an inversion is a deviation from the normal change of an atmospheric property with altitude. It almost always refers to a 'temperature inversion', i.e. an increase in temperature with height, or to the layer ('inversion layer') within which such an increase occurs. An inversion can lead to pollution such as smog being trapped close to the ground, with possible adverse effects on health.

4. Air Temperature

CHAPTER HIGHLIGHTS & NOTES: KEY TERMS, PEOPLE, PLACES, CONCEPTS

Heat index

The heat index or humiture or humidex (not to be confused with the Canadian humidex) is an index that combines air temperature and relative humidity in an attempt to determine the human-perceived equivalent temperature--how hot it would feel if the humidity were some other value. The result is also known as the 'felt air temperature' or 'apparent temperature'. For example, when the temperature is 32 °C (90 °F) with 70% relative humidity, the heat index is 41 °C (106 °F).

Alpine tundra

Alpine tundra is a type of natural region or biome that does not contain trees because it is at high altitude. Alpine tundra is distinguished from arctic tundra, because alpine soils are generally better drained than arctic soils. Alpine tundra transitions to subalpine forests below the tree line; stunted forests occurring at the forest-tundra ecotone are known as Krummholz.

Atlantic

The Atlantic in palaeoclimatology was the warmest and moistest Blytt-Sernander period, pollen zone and chronozone of Holocene northern Europe. The climate was generally warmer than today. It was preceded by the Boreal, with a climate similar to today's, and was followed by the Subboreal, a transition to the modern.

Lapse rate

The lapse rate is defined as the rate of decrease with height for an atmospheric variable. The variable involved is temperature unless specified otherwise. The terminology arises from the word lapse in the sense of a decrease or decline.

Troposphere

The troposphere is the lowest portion of Earth's atmosphere, and is also where all weather takes place. It contains approximately 75% of the atmosphere's mass and 99% of its water vapour and aerosols. The average depths of the troposphere are 20 km (12 mi) in the tropics, 17 km (11 mi) in the mid latitudes, and 7 km (4.3 mi) in the polar regions in winter.

Atmosphere

An atmosphere is a layer of gases surrounding a planet or other material body of sufficient mass that is held in place by the gravity of the body. An atmosphere is more likely to be retained if the gravity is high and the atmosphere's temperature is low.

The atmosphere of Earth, which is mostly nitrogen, also contains oxygen used by most organisms for respiration and carbon dioxide used by plants, algae and cyanobacteria for photosynthesis, also protects living organisms from genetic damage by solar ultraviolet radiation.

Tundra

In physical geography, a tundra is a biome where the tree growth is hindered by low temperatures and short growing seasons. The term tundra comes through Russian ?????? from the Kildin Sami word tundâr 'uplands', 'treeless mountain tract'. There are three types of tundra: arctic tundra, alpine tundra, and antarctic tundra.

Mesosphere

The mesosphere is the layer of the Earth's atmosphere that is directly above the stratopause and directly below the mesopause. In the mesosphere temperature decreases as the altitude increases. The upper boundary of the mesosphere is the mesopause, which can be the coldest naturally occurring place on Earth with temperatures below 130 K (-226 °F; -143 °C).

4. Air Temperature

CHAPTER HIGHLIGHTS & NOTES: KEY TERMS, PEOPLE, PLACES, CONCEPTS

Stratopause

The stratopause is the level of the atmosphere which is the boundary between two layers: the stratosphere and the mesosphere. In the stratosphere the temperature increases with altitude, and the stratopause is the region where a maximum in the temperature occurs. This atmospheric feature is not only associated with Earth: it occurs on any other planet or moon that has an atmosphere as well.

Insolation

Insolation is a measure of solar radiation energy received on a given surface area and recorded during a given time. It is also called solar irradiation and expressed as 'hourly irradiation' if recorded during an hour or 'daily irradiation' if recorded during a day. The unit recommended by the World Meteorological Organization is megajoules per square metre (MJ/m^2) or joules per square millimetre (J/mm^2).

Subsidence

Subsidence in the Earth's atmosphere is most commonly caused by low temperatures: as air cools, it becomes denser and moves towards the ground, just as warm air becomes less dense and moves upwards. Cool subsiding air is subject to adiabatic warming which tends to cause the evaporation of any clouds that might be present. Subsidence generally causes high barometric pressure as more air moves into the same space: the polar highs are areas of almost constant subsidence, as are the horse latitudes, and these areas of subsidence are the sources of much of the world's prevailing wind.

Isothermal

An isothermal process is a change of a system, in which the temperature remains constant: ?T = 0. This typically occurs when a system is in contact with an outside thermal reservoir (heat bath), and the change occurs slowly enough to allow the system to continually adjust to the temperature of the reservoir through heat exchange. In contrast, an adiabatic process is where a system exchanges no heat with its surroundings (Q = 0). In other words, in an isothermal process, the value ?T = 0 and therefore ?U = 0 (only for an ideal gas) but Q ? 0, while in an adiabatic process, ?T ? 0 but Q = 0.

Siberia

Siberia is an extensive geographical region, consisting of almost all of North Asia. Siberia has been part of Russia since the seventeenth century.

The territory of Siberia extends eastwards from the Ural Mountains to the watershed between the Pacific and Arctic drainage basins.

Temperature record

The temperature record shows the fluctuations of the temperature of the atmosphere and the oceans through various spans of time. The most detailed information exists since 1850, when methodical thermometer-based records began. There are numerous estimates of temperatures since the end of the Pleistocene glaciation, particularly during the current Holocene epoch.

Weather satellite

The weather satellite is a type of satellite that is primarily used to monitor the weather and climate of the Earth. Satellites can be polar orbiting, covering the entire Earth asynchronously, or geostationary, hovering over the same spot on the equator.

4. Air Temperature

CHAPTER HIGHLIGHTS & NOTES: KEY TERMS, PEOPLE, PLACES, CONCEPTS

Sea surface temperature	Sea surface temperature is the water temperature close to the ocean's surface. The exact meaning of surface varies according to the measurement method used, but it is between 1 millimetre (0.04 in) and 20 metres (70 ft) below the sea surface. Air masses in the Earth's atmosphere are highly modified by sea surface temperatures within a short distance of the shore.
Coral reef	Coral reefs are underwater structures made from calcium carbonate secreted by corals. Coral reefs are colonies of tiny animals found in marine waters that contain few nutrients. Most coral reefs are built from stony corals, which in turn consist of polyps that cluster in groups.
National Park	A national park is a park in use for conservation purposes. Often it is a reserve of natural, semi-natural, or developed land that a sovereign state declares or owns. Although individual nations designate their own national parks differently, there is a common idea: the conservation of 'wild nature' for posterity and as a symbol of national pride.
Tree	In botany, a tree is a perennial plant with an elongated stem, or trunk, supporting leaves or branches. In some usages, the definition of a tree may be narrower, including only woody plants, only plants that are usable as lumber or only plants above a specified height. At its broadest, trees include the taller palms, the tree ferns, bananas and bamboo.
Coral	Corals are marine invertebrates in class Anthozoa of phylum Cnidaria typically living in compact colonies of many identical individual 'polyps'. The group includes the important reef builders that inhabit tropical oceans and secrete calcium carbonate to form a hard skeleton. A coral 'head' is a colony of myriad genetically identical polyps.
Arctic	The Arctic is a polar region located at the northernmost part of the Earth. The Arctic consists of the Arctic Ocean and parts of Alaska (United States), Canada, Finland, Greenland (Denmark), Iceland, Norway, Russia, and Sweden. The Arctic region consists of a vast ocean with a seasonally varying ice cover, surrounded by treeless permafrost.
Global warming	Global warming is the rise in the average temperature of Earth's atmosphere and oceans since the late 19th century and its projected continuation. Since the early 20th century, Earth's mean surface temperature has increased by about 0.8 °C (1.4 °F), with about two-thirds of the increase occurring since 1980. Warming of the climate system is unequivocal, and scientists are 95-100% certain that it is primarily caused by increasing concentrations of greenhouse gases produced by human activities such as the burning of fossil fuels and deforestation. These findings are recognized by the national science academies of all major industrialized nations.

4. Air Temperature

Climate	Climate is a measure of the average pattern of variation in temperature, humidity, atmospheric pressure, wind, precipitation, atmospheric particle count and other meteorological variables in a given region over long periods of time. Climate is different than weather, in that weather only describes the short-term conditions of these variables in a given region. A region's climate is generated by the climate system, which has five components: atmosphere, hydrosphere, cryosphere, land surface, and biosphere.
Lithosphere	The lithosphere is the rigid outermost shell of a rocky planet defined on the basis of the mechanical properties. On Earth, it comprises the crust and the portion of the upper mantle that behaves elastically on time scales of thousands of years or greater. The outermost shell of a rocky planet defined on the basis of the chemistry and mineralogy is a crust.
Sea-level rise	Sea level rise has been estimated to be on average between +2.6 millimetres and 2.9 millimetres (0.11 in) per year ± 0.4 millimetres (0.016 in) since 1993. Additionally, sea level rise has accelerated in recent years. For the period between 1870 and 2004, global average sea levels are estimated to have risen a total of 195 millimetres (7.7 in), and 1.7 millimetres (0.067 in) ± 0.3 millimetres (0.012 in) per year, with a significant acceleration of sea-level rise of 0.013 millimetres (0.00051 in) ± 0.006 millimetres (0.00024 in) per year per year.
Sea ice	Sea ice arises as seawater freezes. Because ice is less dense than water, it floats on the ocean's surface (as does fresh water ice, which has an even lower density). Sea ice covers about 7% of the Earth's surface and about 12% of the world's oceans.
Ecosystem	An ecosystem is a community of living organisms in conjunction with the nonliving components of their environment (things like air, water and mineral soil), interacting as a system. These biotic and abiotic components are regarded as linked together through nutrient cycles and energy flows. As ecosystems are defined by the network of interactions among organisms, and between organisms and their environment, they can be of any size but usually encompass specific, limited spaces (although some scientists say that the entire planet is an ecosystem).
Habitat	A habitat is an ecological or environmental area that is inhabited by a particular species of animal, plant, or other type of organism. The term typically refers to the zone in which the organism lives and where it can find food, shelter, protection and mates for reproduction, utilizing the qualities the species has adapted to survive within the ecology of the habitat. It is the natural environment in which an organism lives, or the physical environment that surrounds a species population.
Kyoto Protocol	The Kyoto Protocol to the United Nations Framework Convention on Climate Change is an international treaty that sets binding obligations on industrialized countries to reduce emissions of greenhouse gases. The UNFCCC is an environmental treaty with the goal of preventing 'dangerous' anthropogenic (i.e., human-induced) interference of the climate system.

4. Air Temperature

CHAPTER HIGHLIGHTS & NOTES: KEY TERMS, PEOPLE, PLACES, CONCEPTS

Greenhouse gas	A greenhouse gas is a gas in an atmosphere that absorbs and emits radiation within the thermal infrared range. This process is the fundamental cause of the greenhouse effect. The primary greenhouse gases in the Earth's atmosphere are water vapor, carbon dioxide, methane, nitrous oxide, and ozone.

CHAPTER QUIZ: KEY TERMS, PEOPLE, PLACES, CONCEPTS

1. _________ is a type of natural region or biome that does not contain trees because it is at high altitude. _________ is distinguished from arctic tundra, because alpine soils are generally better drained than arctic soils. _________ transitions to subalpine forests below the tree line; stunted forests occurring at the forest-tundra ecotone are known as Krummholz.

   a. Teniente Luis Carvajal Villaroel Antarctic Base
   b. West Antarctica
   c. Alpine tundra
   d. Bellingshausen Sea

2. The _________ of a geographic location is its height above a fixed reference point, most commonly a reference geoid, a mathematical model of the Earth's sea level as an equipotential gravitational surface . _________, or geometric height, is mainly used when referring to points on the Earth's surface, while altitude or geopotential height is used for points above the surface, such as an aircraft in flight or a spacecraft in orbit, and depth is used for points below the surface.

   Less commonly, _________ is measured using the center of the Earth as the reference point.

   a. Bathymetric chart
   b. Bridge scour
   c. British Society for Geomorphology
   d. Elevation

3. An _________ is a metropolitan area that is significantly warmer than its surrounding rural areas due to human activities. The phenomenon was first investigated and described by Luke Howard in the 1810s, although he was not the one to name the phenomenon. The temperature difference usually is larger at night than during the day, and is most apparent when winds are weak.

   a. Berkeley Earth
   b. Climate commitment
   c. Urban heat island
   d. Climate Science Rapid Response Team

4. . _________ is the study of the distribution of species and ecosystems in geographic space and through geological time.

Organisms and biological communities vary in a highly regular fashion along geographic gradients of latitude, elevation, isolation and habitat area.

Knowledge of spatial variation in the numbers and types of organisms is as vital to us today as it was to our early human ancestors, as we adapt to heterogeneous but geographically predictable environments.

a. Teniente Luis Carvajal Villaroel Antarctic Base
b. Biogeography
c. British Antarctic Territory
d. Bellingshausen Sea

5. The _________ is the rigid outermost shell of a rocky planet defined on the basis of the mechanical properties. On Earth, it comprises the crust and the portion of the upper mantle that behaves elastically on time scales of thousands of years or greater. The outermost shell of a rocky planet defined on the basis of the chemistry and mineralogy is a crust.

a. Bathymetric chart
b. Bridge scour
c. British Society for Geomorphology
d. Lithosphere

ANSWER KEY
4. Air Temperature

1. c
2. d
3. c
4. b
5. d

5. Atmospheric Moisture and Precipitation

CHAPTER OUTLINE: KEY TERMS, PEOPLE, PLACES, CONCEPTS

- Island
- Acid rain
- Weathering
- Ice age
- Latent Heat
- Specific heat
- Surface tension
- Ocean current
- Precambrian
- Hydrosphere
- Habitat
- Subsidence
- Humidity
- Adiabatic
- Cloud
- Geo
- Convective precipitation
- Cyclonic
- Rain gauge
- Rain shadow
- Unstable

5. Atmospheric Moisture and Precipitation

CHAPTER OUTLINE: KEY TERMS, PEOPLE, PLACES, CONCEPTS

- Accretion
- Freezing rain
- River
- Climate change
- Radiometric dating
- Air-mass thunderstorm
- Climograph
- Hurricane Katrina
- Mesoscale convective system
- Thunderstorm
- Weather radar
- National Park
- Serengeti
- Tanzania
- Wind
- Wind shear
- Derecho
- Squall line
- Enhanced Fujita
- Fallout
- Smog

5. Atmospheric Moisture and Precipitation

CHAPTER HIGHLIGHTS & NOTES: KEY TERMS, PEOPLE, PLACES, CONCEPTS

Island	An island or isle is any piece of sub-continental land that is surrounded by water. Very small islands such as emergent land features on atolls can be called islets, skerries, cays or keys. An island in a river or a lake island may be called an eyot or ait, or a holm.
Acid rain	Acid rain is a rain or any other form of precipitation that is unusually acidic, meaning that it possesses elevated levels of hydrogen ions . It can have harmful effects on plants, aquatic animals and infrastructure. Acid rain is caused by emissions of sulfur dioxide and nitrogen oxide, which react with the water molecules in the atmosphere to produce acids.
Weathering	Weathering is the breaking down of rocks, soil and minerals as well as artificial materials through contact with the Earth's atmosphere, biota and waters. Weathering occurs in situ, roughly translated to: 'with no movement', and thus should not be confused with erosion, which involves the movement of rocks and minerals by agents such as water, ice, snow, wind, waves and gravity and then being transported and deposited in other locations. Two important classifications of weathering processes exist - physical and chemical weathering; each sometimes involves a biological component.
Ice age	An ice age, or more precisely, a glacial age, is a period of long-term reduction in the temperature of the Earth's surface and atmosphere, resulting in the presence or expansion of continental and polar ice sheets and alpine glaciers. Within a long-term ice age, individual pulses of cold climate are termed 'glacial periods' (or alternatively 'glacials' or 'glaciations' or colloquially as 'ice age'), and intermittent warm periods are called 'interglacials'. Glaciologically, ice age implies the presence of extensive ice sheets in the northern and southern hemispheres.
Latent Heat	Latent heat is energy released or absorbed, by a body or a thermodynamic system, during a constant-temperature process that is specified in some way. An example is latent heat of fusion for a phase change, melting, at a specified temperature and pressure. The term was introduced around 1762 by Scottish chemist Joseph Black.
Specific heat	Heat capacity or thermal capacity is a measurable physical quantity equal to the ratio of the heat added to an object to the resulting temperature change. The SI unit of heat capacity is joule per kelvin $\frac{J}{K}$ and the dimensional form is $L^2MT^{-2}T^{-1}$. Specific heat is the amount of heat needed to raise the temperature of one gram of mass by 1 degree Celsius.
Surface tension	Surface tension is the elastic tendency of a fluid surface which makes it acquire the least surface area possible. Surface tension allows insects (e.g. water striders), usually denser than water, to float and stride on a water surface. At liquid-air interfaces, surface tension results from the greater attraction of liquid molecules to each other (due to cohesion) than to the molecules in the air (due to adhesion).

Ocean current	An ocean current is a continuous, directed movement of seawater generated by the forces acting upon this mean flow, such as breaking waves, wind, Coriolis effect, cabbeling, temperature and salinity differences and tides caused by the gravitational pull of the Moon and the Sun. Depth contours, shoreline configurations and interaction with other currents influence a current's direction and strength. A deep current is any ocean current at a depth of greater than 100m.
Precambrian	The Precambrian or Pre-Cambrian, sometimes abbreviated p?, is the largest span of time in Earth's history before the current Phanerozoic Eon, and is a Supereon divided into several eons of the geologic time scale. It spans from the formation of Earth about 4.6 billion years ago (Ga) to the beginning of the Cambrian Period, about 541 million years ago (Ma), when hard-shelled creatures first appeared in abundance. The Precambrian is so named because it precedes the Cambrian, the first period of the Phanerozoic Eon, which is named after Cambria, the classical name for Wales, where rocks from this age were first studied.
Hydrosphere	The hydrosphere in physical geography describes the combined mass of water found on, under, and over the surface of a planet. Igor Shiklomanov, the man selected by the United Nations to do its world inventory of water resources, estimated that there are 1386 million cubic kilometres of water on earth. This includes water in liquid and frozen forms in groundwaters, glaciers, oceans, lakes and streams.
Habitat	A habitat is an ecological or environmental area that is inhabited by a particular species of animal, plant, or other type of organism. The term typically refers to the zone in which the organism lives and where it can find food, shelter, protection and mates for reproduction, utilizing the qualities the species has adapted to survive within the ecology of the habitat. It is the natural environment in which an organism lives, or the physical environment that surrounds a species population.
Subsidence	Subsidence in the Earth's atmosphere is most commonly caused by low temperatures: as air cools, it becomes denser and moves towards the ground, just as warm air becomes less dense and moves upwards. Cool subsiding air is subject to adiabatic warming which tends to cause the evaporation of any clouds that might be present. Subsidence generally causes high barometric pressure as more air moves into the same space: the polar highs are areas of almost constant subsidence, as are the horse latitudes, and these areas of subsidence are the sources of much of the world's prevailing wind.
Humidity	Humidity is the amount of water vapor in the air. Water vapor is the gaseous state of water and is invisible. Humidity indicates the likelihood of precipitation, dew, or fog.
Adiabatic	An adiabatic process is one that occurs without transfer of heat or matter between a thermodynamic system and its surroundings. In an adiabatic process, energy is transferred only as work.

5. Atmospheric Moisture and Precipitation

CHAPTER HIGHLIGHTS & NOTES: KEY TERMS, PEOPLE, PLACES, CONCEPTS

Cloud	In meteorology, a cloud is a visible mass of liquid droplets or frozen crystals made of water or various chemicals suspended in the atmosphere above the surface of a planetary body. These suspended particles are also known as aerosols and are studied in the cloud physics branch of meteorology. Terrestrial cloud formation is the result of air in Earth's atmosphere becoming saturated due to either or both of two processes; cooling of the air and adding water vapor.
Geo	A geo or gio is an inlet, a gully or a narrow and deep cleft in the face of a cliff. Geos are common on the coastline of the Shetland and Orkney islands. They are created by the wave driven erosion of cliffs along faults and bedding planes in the rock.
Convective precipitation	In meteorology, 'precipitation types' can include the character or phase of the precipitation which is falling to ground level. There are three distinct ways that precipitation can occur. Convective precipitation is generally more intense, and of shorter duration, than stratiform precipitation.
Cyclonic	In meteorology, a cyclone is a large scale air mass that rotates around a strong center of low pressure. They is usually characterized by inward spiraling winds that rotate counterclockwise in the Northern Hemisphere and clockwise in the Southern Hemisphere of the Earth. All large-scale cyclonic circulations are centered on areas of low atmospheric pressure.
Rain gauge	A rain gauge is a type of instrument used by meteorologists and hydrologists to gather and measure the amount of liquid precipitation over a set period of time.
Rain shadow	A rain shadow is a dry area on the lee side of a mountainous area . The mountains block the passage of rain-producing weather systems and cast a 'pencil' of dryness behind them. As shown by the diagram to the right, the incoming warm and moist air is drawn by the prevailing winds towards the top of the mountains, where it condenses and precipitates before it crosses the top.
Unstable	In numerous fields of study, the component of instability within a system is generally characterized by some of the outputs or internal states growing without bounds. Not all systems that are not stable are unstable; systems can also be marginally stable or exhibit limit cycle behavior. In structural engineering, a structure can become unstable when excessive load is applied.
Accretion	Accretion is the process of coastal sediment returning to the visible portion of a beach or foreshore following a submersion event. A sustainable beach or foreshore often goes through a cycle of submersion during rough weather then accretion during calmer periods. If a coastline is not in a healthy sustainable state, then erosion can be more serious and accretion does not fully restore the original volume of the visible beach or foreshore leading to permanent beach loss.

Freezing rain	Freezing rain is the name given to rain that falls when surface temperatures are below freezing. Unlike a mixture of rain and snow, ice pellets (both of which are sometimes called 'sleet'), or hail, freezing rain is made entirely of liquid droplets. The raindrops become supercooled while passing through a sub-freezing layer of air hundreds of meters above the ground, and then freeze upon impact with any surface they encounter.
River	A river is a natural watercourse, usually freshwater, flowing towards an ocean, a lake, a sea, or another river. In a few cases, a river simply flows into the ground or dries up completely at the end of its course, and does not reach another body of water. Small rivers may be called by several other names, including stream, creek, brook, rivulet, and rill.
Climate change	Climate change is a significant and lasting change in the statistical distribution of weather patterns over periods ranging from decades to millions of years. It may be a change in average weather conditions, or in the distribution of weather around the average conditions (i.e., more or fewer extreme weather events). Climate change is caused by factors such as biotic processes, variations in solar radiation received by Earth, plate tectonics, and volcanic eruptions.
Radiometric dating	Radiometric dating or radioactive dating is a technique used to date materials such as rocks or carbon, in which trace radioactive impurities were selectively incorporated when they formed. The method compares the abundance of a naturally occurring radioactive isotope within the material to the abundance of its decay products, which form at a known constant rate of decay. The use of radiometric dating was first published in 1907 by Bertram Boltwood and is now the principal source of information about the absolute age of rocks and other geological features, including the age of the Earth itself, and can be used to date a wide range of natural and man-made materials.
Air-mass thunderstorm	An air-mass thunderstorm, also called an 'ordinary', 'single cell', or 'garden variety' thunderstorm, is a thunderstorm that is generally weak and usually not severe. These storms form in environments where at least some amount of Convective Available Potential Energy (CAPE) is present, but very low levels of wind shear and helicity. The lifting source, which is a crucial factor in thunderstorm development, is usually the result of uneven heating of the surface, though they can be induced by weather fronts and other low-level boundaries associated with wind convergence.
Climograph	A climograph is a graphical representation of basic climatic parameters, that is monthly average temperature and precipitation, at a certain location. It is used for a quick-view of the climate of a location.
Hurricane Katrina	Hurricane Katrina was the deadliest and most destructive Atlantic tropical cyclone of the 2005 Atlantic hurricane season. It is the costliest natural disaster, as well as one of the five deadliest hurricanes, in the history of the United States. Katrina is the seventh most intense Atlantic hurricane ever recorded, part of the 2005 season that included three of the six most intense Atlantic hurricanes ever documented (along with #1 Wilma and #4 Rita).

5. Atmospheric Moisture and Precipitation

CHAPTER HIGHLIGHTS & NOTES: KEY TERMS, PEOPLE, PLACES, CONCEPTS

Mesoscale convective system	A mesoscale convective system is a complex of thunderstorms that becomes organized on a scale larger than the individual thunderstorms but smaller than extratropical cyclones, and normally persists for several hours or more. A mesoscale convective system's overall cloud and precipitation pattern may be round or linear in shape, and include weather systems such as tropical cyclones, squall lines, lake-effect snow events, polar lows, and Mesoscale Convective Complexes (MCCs), and generally form near weather fronts. The type that forms during the warm season over land has been noted across North America, Europe, and Asia, with a maximum in activity noted during the late afternoon and evening hours.
Thunderstorm	A thunderstorm, also known as an electrical storm, a lightning storm, thundershower or simply a storm, is a form of turbulent weather characterized by the presence of lightning and its acoustic effect on the Earth's atmosphere known as thunder. The meteorologically assigned cloud type associated with the thunderstorm is the cumulonimbus. Thunderstorms are usually accompanied by strong winds, heavy rain and sometimes snow, sleet, hail, or no precipitation at all.
Weather radar	Weather radar, also called weather surveillance radar and Doppler weather radar, is a type of radar used to locate precipitation, calculate its motion, and estimate its type (rain, snow, hail etc).. Modern weather radars are mostly pulse-Doppler radars, capable of detecting the motion of rain droplets in addition to the intensity of the precipitation. Both types of data can be analyzed to determine the structure of storms and their potential to cause severe weather.
National Park	A national park is a park in use for conservation purposes. Often it is a reserve of natural, semi-natural, or developed land that a sovereign state declares or owns. Although individual nations designate their own national parks differently, there is a common idea: the conservation of 'wild nature' for posterity and as a symbol of national pride.
Serengeti	The Serengeti ecosystem is a geographical region in Africa. It is located in north Tanzania and extends to south-western Kenya between latitudes 1 and 3 degrees south latitude and 34 and 36 degrees east longitude. It spans some 30,000 km^2 (12,000 sq mi). The Kenyan part of the Serengeti is known as Maasai (Masai) Mara.
Tanzania	Tanzania, officially the United Republic of Tanzania, is a country in East Africa in the African Great Lakes region. It is bordered by Kenya and Uganda to the north; Rwanda, Burundi, and the Democratic Republic of the Congo to the west; and Zambia, Malawi, and Mozambique to the south. The country's eastern border is formed by the Indian Ocean.
Wind	Wind is the flow of gases on a large scale. On the surface of the Earth, wind consists of the bulk movement of air. In outer space, solar wind is the movement of gases or charged particles from the sun through space, while planetary wind is the outgassing of light chemical elements from a planet's atmosphere into space.

Wind shear

Wind shear, sometimes referred to as windshear or wind gradient, is a difference in wind speed and direction over a relatively short distance in the atmosphere. Wind shear can be broken down into vertical and horizontal components, with horizontal wind shear seen across fronts and near the coast, and vertical shear typically near the surface, though also at higher levels in the atmosphere near upper level jets and frontal zones aloft.

Wind shear itself is a microscale meteorological phenomenon occurring over a very small distance, but it can be associated with mesoscale or synoptic scale weather features such as squall lines and cold fronts.

Derecho

A derecho is a widespread, long-lived, straight-line wind storm that is associated with a land-based, fast-moving group of severe thunderstorms.

Derechos can cause hurricane force winds, tornadoes, heavy rains, and flash floods. Convection-induced winds take on a bow echo (backward 'C') form of squall line, forming in an area of wind divergence in upper levels of the troposphere, within a region of low-level warm air advection and rich low-level moisture. They travel quickly in the direction of movement of their associated storms, similar to an outflow boundary (gust front), except that the wind is sustained and increases in strength behind the front, generally exceeding hurricane-force.

Squall line

A squall line is a line of thunderstorms that can form along or ahead of a cold front. In the early 20th century, the term was used as a synonym for cold front. It contains heavy precipitation, hail, frequent lightning, strong straight-line winds, and possibly tornadoes and waterspouts.

Enhanced Fujita

The Enhanced Fujita scale rates the strength of tornadoes in the United States and Canada based on the damage they cause.

Implemented in place of the Fujita scale introduced in 1971 by Tetsuya Theodore Fujita, it began operational use in the United States on February 1, 2007, followed by Canada on April 1, 2013. The scale has the same basic design as the original Fujita scale--six categories from zero to five, representing increasing degrees of damage. It was revised to reflect better examinations of tornado damage surveys, so as to align wind speeds more closely with associated storm damage.

Fallout

Nuclear fallout, or simply fallout, is the residual radioactive material propelled into the upper atmosphere following a nuclear blast or a nuclear reaction conducted in an unshielded facility, so called because it 'falls out' of the sky after the explosion and the shock wave have passed. It commonly refers to the radioactive dust and ash created when a nuclear weapon explodes, but such dust can also originate from a damaged nuclear plant. Fallout may take the form of black rain (rain darkened by particulates).

Smog

Smog is a type of air pollutant. The word 'smog' was coined in the early 20th century as a portmanteau of the words smoke and fog to refer to smoky fog.

5. Atmospheric Moisture and Precipitation

CHAPTER QUIZ: KEY TERMS, PEOPLE, PLACES, CONCEPTS

1. The _________ ecosystem is a geographical region in Africa. It is located in north Tanzania and extends to south-western Kenya between latitudes 1 and 3 degrees south latitude and 34 and 36 degrees east longitude. It spans some 30,000 km^2 (12,000 sq mi). The Kenyan part of the _________ is known as Maasai (Masai) Mara.

   a. Serengeti
   b. Kaokoveld
   c. Lake Natron
   d. Mandara Plateau mosaic

2. _________ is a type of air pollutant. The word '_________' was coined in the early 20th century as a portmanteau of the words smoke and fog to refer to smoky fog. The word was then intended to refer to what was sometimes known as pea soup fog, a familiar and serious problem in London from the 19th century to the mid 20th century.

   a. Mughal Empire
   b. Thunderstorm
   c. Wind gradient
   d. Smog

3. A _________ is a widespread, long-lived, straight-line wind storm that is associated with a land-based, fast-moving group of severe thunderstorms.

   _________s can cause hurricane force winds, tornadoes, heavy rains, and flash floods. Convection-induced winds take on a bow echo (backward 'C') form of squall line, forming in an area of wind divergence in upper levels of the troposphere, within a region of low-level warm air advection and rich low-level moisture. They travel quickly in the direction of movement of their associated storms, similar to an outflow boundary (gust front), except that the wind is sustained and increases in strength behind the front, generally exceeding hurricane-force.

   a. Mughal Empire
   b. Derecho
   c. Wind gradient
   d. Teniente Luis Carvajal Villaroel Antarctic Base

4. A _________ is an ecological or environmental area that is inhabited by a particular species of animal, plant, or other type of organism. The term typically refers to the zone in which the organism lives and where it can find food, shelter, protection and mates for reproduction, utilizing the qualities the species has adapted to survive within the ecology of the _________. It is the natural environment in which an organism lives, or the physical environment that surrounds a species population.

   a. Mughal Empire
   b. Bridge scour
   c. British Society for Geomorphology
   d. Habitat

5. _________ is a rain or any other form of precipitation that is unusually acidic, meaning that it possesses elevated levels of hydrogen ions . It can have harmful effects on plants, aquatic animals and infrastructure. _________ is caused by emissions of sulfur dioxide and nitrogen oxide, which react with the water molecules in the atmosphere to produce acids.

a. Acid rain
b. West Antarctica
c. British Antarctic Territory
d. Bellingshausen Sea

ANSWER KEY
5. Atmospheric Moisture and Precipitation

---

1. a
2. d
3. b
4. d
5. a

---

6. Winds and Global Circulation

CHAPTER OUTLINE: KEY TERMS, PEOPLE, PLACES, CONCEPTS

Antarctica

Wind

Humboldt Current

Barometer

Atmospheric pressure

Alpine tundra

Radiometric dating

Altitude

Tundra

Anemometer

Pressure gradient

Land

Anticyclone

Cyclone

Polar easterlies

Trade wind

Azores High

Monsoon

Polar high

Atmosphere

Geostrophic

6. Winds and Global Circulation

CHAPTER OUTLINE: KEY TERMS, PEOPLE, PLACES, CONCEPTS

________	Jet stream
________	Middle East
________	Ocean
________	Ocean current
________	North Atlantic oscillation
________	Deep ocean
________	Thermohaline circulation

CHAPTER HIGHLIGHTS & NOTES: KEY TERMS, PEOPLE, PLACES, CONCEPTS

Antarctica
Antarctica is Earth's southernmost continent, containing the geographic South Pole. It is situated in the Antarctic region of the Southern Hemisphere, almost entirely south of the Antarctic Circle, and is surrounded by the Southern Ocean. At 14.0 million km^2 (5.4 million sq mi), it is the fifth-largest continent in area after Asia, Africa, North America, and South America. For comparison, Antarctica is nearly twice the size of Australia.

Wind
Wind is the flow of gases on a large scale. On the surface of the Earth, wind consists of the bulk movement of air. In outer space, solar wind is the movement of gases or charged particles from the sun through space, while planetary wind is the outgassing of light chemical elements from a planet's atmosphere into space.

Humboldt Current
The Humboldt Current is a cold, low-salinity ocean current that flows north along the west coast of South America from the southern tip of Chile to northern Peru. Also called the Peru Current, it is an eastern boundary current flowing in the direction of the equator, and can extend 1,000 kilometers offshore. The Humboldt Current Large Marine Ecosystem (LME) is one of the major upwelling systems of the world, supporting an extraordinary abundance of marine life.

Barometer
A barometer is a scientific instrument used in meteorology to measure atmospheric pressure. Pressure tendency can forecast short term changes in the weather.

6. Winds and Global Circulation

Atmospheric pressure	Atmospheric pressure, sometimes also called barometric pressure, is the pressure exerted by the weight of air in the atmosphere of Earth . In most circumstances atmospheric pressure is closely approximated by the hydrostatic pressure caused by the weight of air above the measurement point. Low-pressure areas have less atmospheric mass above their location, whereas high-pressure areas have more atmospheric mass above their location.
Alpine tundra	Alpine tundra is a type of natural region or biome that does not contain trees because it is at high altitude. Alpine tundra is distinguished from arctic tundra, because alpine soils are generally better drained than arctic soils. Alpine tundra transitions to subalpine forests below the tree line; stunted forests occurring at the forest-tundra ecotone are known as Krummholz.
Radiometric dating	Radiometric dating or radioactive dating is a technique used to date materials such as rocks or carbon, in which trace radioactive impurities were selectively incorporated when they formed. The method compares the abundance of a naturally occurring radioactive isotope within the material to the abundance of its decay products, which form at a known constant rate of decay. The use of radiometric dating was first published in 1907 by Bertram Boltwood and is now the principal source of information about the absolute age of rocks and other geological features, including the age of the Earth itself, and can be used to date a wide range of natural and man-made materials.
Altitude	Altitude or height is defined based on the context in which it is used . As a general definition, altitude is a distance measurement, usually in the vertical or 'up' direction, between a reference datum and a point or object. The reference datum also often varies according to the context.
Tundra	In physical geography, a tundra is a biome where the tree growth is hindered by low temperatures and short growing seasons. The term tundra comes through Russian ?????? from the Kildin Sami word tundâr 'uplands', 'treeless mountain tract'. There are three types of tundra: arctic tundra, alpine tundra, and antarctic tundra.
Anemometer	An anemometer is a device used for measuring wind speed, and is a common weather station instrument. The term is derived from the Greek word anemos, meaning wind, and is used to describe any airspeed measurement instrument used in meteorology or aerodynamics. The first known description of an anemometer was given by Leon Battista Alberti around 1450.
Pressure gradient	In atmospheric sciences, the pressure gradient is a physical quantity that describes which direction and at what rate the pressure changes the most rapidly around a particular location. The pressure gradient is a dimensional quantity expressed in units of pressure per unit length, or Pa/m. Mathematically, it is obtained by applying the del operator to a pressure function of position.
Land	Land, sometimes referred to as dry land, is the solid surface of the Earth, that is not covered by water. The division between land and ocean, sea, or other bodies of water, is one of the most fundamental separations on the planet.

6. Winds and Global Circulation

CHAPTER HIGHLIGHTS & NOTES: KEY TERMS, PEOPLE, PLACES, CONCEPTS

Anticyclone	An anticyclone is a weather phenomenon defined by the United States' National Weather Service's glossary as '[a] large-scale circulation of winds around a central region of high atmospheric pressure, clockwise in the Northern Hemisphere, counterclockwise in the Southern Hemisphere'. Effects of surface-based anticyclones include clearing skies as well as cooler, drier air. Fog can also form overnight within a region of higher pressure.
Cyclone	In meteorology, a cyclone is an area of closed, circular fluid motion rotating in the same direction as the Earth. This is usually characterized by inward spiraling winds that rotate anti-clockwise in the Northern Hemisphere and clockwise in the Southern Hemisphere of the Earth. Most large-scale cyclonic circulations are centered on areas of low atmospheric pressure.
Polar easterlies	The polar easterlies are the dry, cold prevailing winds that blow from the high-pressure areas of the polar highs at the north and south poles towards low-pressure areas within the Westerlies at high latitudes. Cold air subsides at the pole creating the high pressure, forcing an equatorward outflow of air; that outflow is then deflected westward by the Coriolis effect. Unlike the westerlies in the middle latitudes, the polar easterlies are often weak and irregular.
Trade wind	The trade winds are the prevailing pattern of easterly surface winds found in the tropics, within the lower portion of the Earth's atmosphere, in the lower section of the troposphere near the Earth's equator. The trade winds blow predominantly from the northeast in the Northern Hemisphere and from the southeast in the Southern Hemisphere, strengthening during the winter and when the Arctic oscillation is in its warm phase. Historically, the trade winds have been used by captains of sailing ships to cross the world's oceans for centuries, and enabled European empire expansion into the Americas and trade routes to become established across the Atlantic and Pacific oceans, however, this is not where the term 'trade' originates.
Azores High	The Azores High is a large subtropical semi-permanent centre of high atmospheric pressure typically found south of the Azores in the Atlantic Ocean, at the Horse latitudes. It forms one pole of the North Atlantic oscillation, the other being the Icelandic Low. The system influences the weather and climatic patterns of vast areas of North Africa and Europe, and to a lesser extent, eastern North America. The aridity of the Sahara Desert and Mediterranean Basin is due to the subsidence of air in the system.
Monsoon	Monsoon is traditionally defined as a seasonal reversing wind accompanied by corresponding changes in precipitation, but is now used to describe seasonal changes in atmospheric circulation and precipitation associated with the asymmetric heating of land and sea. Usually, the term monsoon is used to refer to the rainy phase of a seasonally-changing pattern, although technically there is also a dry phase. The major monsoon systems of the world consist of the West African and Asia-Australian monsoons.

Polar high

The polar highs are areas of high atmospheric pressure around the north and south poles, south polar high being the stronger one because land gains and loses heat more effectively than sea. The cold temperatures in the polar regions cause air to descend to create the high pressure (a process called subsidence), just as the warm temperatures around the equator cause air to rise to create the low pressure doldrums. Closely related to this concept is the polar vortex.

Atmosphere

An atmosphere is a layer of gases surrounding a planet or other material body of sufficient mass that is held in place by the gravity of the body. An atmosphere is more likely to be retained if the gravity is high and the atmosphere's temperature is low.

The atmosphere of Earth, which is mostly nitrogen, also contains oxygen used by most organisms for respiration and carbon dioxide used by plants, algae and cyanobacteria for photosynthesis, also protects living organisms from genetic damage by solar ultraviolet radiation.

Geostrophic

A geostrophic current is an oceanic flow in which the pressure gradient force is balanced by the Coriolis effect. The direction of geostrophic flow is parallel to the isobars, with the high pressure to the right of the flow in the Northern Hemisphere, and the high pressure to the left in the Southern Hemisphere. This concept is familiar from weather maps, whose isobars show the direction of geostrophic flow in the atmosphere.

Jet stream

Jet streams are fast flowing, narrow, meandering, air currents found in the upper atmosphere or in troposphere of some planets, including Earth. The main jet streams are located near the altitude of the tropopause. The major jet streams on Earth are westerly winds (flowing west to east).

Middle East

The Middle East is a region that roughly encompasses a majority of Western Asia (excluding the Caucasus) and Egypt. The term is used as a synonym for Near East, in opposition to Far East. The corresponding adjective is Middle Eastern and the derived noun is Middle Easterner.

Ocean

An ocean is a body of saline water that composes much of a planet's hydrosphere. On Earth, an ocean is one or all of the major divisions of the planet's World Ocean - which are, in descending order of area, the Pacific, Atlantic, Indian, Southern (Antarctic), and Arctic Oceans. The word sea is often used interchangeably with 'ocean' in American English but, strictly speaking, a sea is a body of saline water (generally a division of the World Ocean) that land partly or fully encloses.

Ocean current

An ocean current is a continuous, directed movement of seawater generated by the forces acting upon this mean flow, such as breaking waves, wind, Coriolis effect, cabbeling, temperature and salinity differences and tides caused by the gravitational pull of the Moon and the Sun. Depth contours, shoreline configurations and interaction with other currents influence a current's direction and strength. A deep current is any ocean current at a depth of greater than 100m.

6. Winds and Global Circulation

CHAPTER HIGHLIGHTS & NOTES: KEY TERMS, PEOPLE, PLACES, CONCEPTS

North Atlantic oscillation	The North Atlantic Oscillation is a climatic phenomenon in the North Atlantic Ocean of fluctuations in the difference of atmospheric pressure at sea level between the Icelandic low and the Azores high. Through east-west oscillation motions of the Icelandic low and the Azores high, it controls the strength and direction of westerly winds and storm tracks across the North Atlantic. It is part of the Arctic oscillation, and varies over time with no particular periodicity.
Deep ocean	The deep sea or deep layer is the lowest layer in the ocean, existing below the thermocline and above the seabed, at a depth of 1000 fathoms or more. Little or no light penetrates this part of the ocean, and most of the organisms that live there rely for subsistence on falling organic matter produced in the photic zone. For this reason, scientists once assumed that life would be sparse in the deep ocean, but virtually every probe has revealed that, on the contrary, life is abundant in the deep ocean.
Thermohaline circulation	Thermohaline circulation is a part of the large-scale ocean circulation that is driven by global density gradients created by surface heat and freshwater fluxes. The adjective thermohaline derives from thermo- referring to temperature and -haline referring to salt content, factors which together determine the density of sea water. Wind-driven surface currents (such as the Gulf Stream) travel polewards from the equatorial Atlantic Ocean, cooling en route, and eventually sinking at high latitudes (forming North Atlantic Deep Water).

CHAPTER QUIZ: KEY TERMS, PEOPLE, PLACES, CONCEPTS

1. In physical geography, a _________ is a biome where the tree growth is hindered by low temperatures and short growing seasons. The term _________ comes through Russian ?????? from the Kildin Sami word tundâr 'uplands', 'treeless mountain tract'. There are three types of _________: arctic _________, alpine _________, and antarctic _________.

    a. Mangrove
    b. Tundra
    c. Mediterranean forests, woodlands, and scrub
    d. Mire

2. . In atmospheric sciences, the _________ is a physical quantity that describes which direction and at what rate the pressure changes the most rapidly around a particular location. The _________ is a dimensional quantity expressed in units of pressure per unit length, or Pa/m.

    Mathematically, it is obtained by applying the del operator to a pressure function of position.

    a. Baroclinic
    b. Mughal Empire

c. Russian Empire
d. Pressure gradient

3. _________s are fast flowing, narrow, meandering, air currents found in the upper atmosphere or in troposphere of some planets, including Earth. The main _________s are located near the altitude of the tropopause. The major _________s on Earth are westerly winds (flowing west to east).

a. Mughal Empire
b. Jet stream
c. Bond event
d. Climate classification

4. _________ is Earth's southernmost continent, containing the geographic South Pole. It is situated in the Antarctic region of the Southern Hemisphere, almost entirely south of the Antarctic Circle, and is surrounded by the Southern Ocean. At 14.0 million km^2 (5.4 million sq mi), it is the fifth-largest continent in area after Asia, Africa, North America, and South America. For comparison, _________ is nearly twice the size of Australia.

a. Water hemisphere
b. Land hemisphere
c. Australian Antarctic Territory
d. Antarctica

5. An _________ is a device used for measuring wind speed, and is a common weather station instrument. The term is derived from the Greek word anemos, meaning wind, and is used to describe any airspeed measurement instrument used in meteorology or aerodynamics. The first known description of an _________ was given by Leon Battista Alberti around 1450.

a. Teniente Luis Carvajal Villaroel Antarctic Base
b. Anemometer
c. British Antarctic Territory
d. Bellingshausen Sea

ANSWER KEY
6. Winds and Global Circulation

---

1. b
2. d
3. b
4. d
5. b

---

7. Weather Systems

CHAPTER OUTLINE: KEY TERMS, PEOPLE, PLACES, CONCEPTS

- Climograph
- Precambrian
- Climate
- Cloud
- Cloud cover
- Precipitation
- Cyclone
- Desert
- Latitude
- Pressure gradient
- Wind
- Air mass
- Cold front
- Overland flow
- Dry line
- Anticyclone
- Trough
- Tropical cyclone
- Radiometric dating
- Storm surge
- Hurricane Katrina

Thermohaline circulation

CHAPTER HIGHLIGHTS & NOTES: KEY TERMS, PEOPLE, PLACES, CONCEPTS

Climograph

A climograph is a graphical representation of basic climatic parameters, that is monthly average temperature and precipitation, at a certain location. It is used for a quick-view of the climate of a location.

Precambrian

The Precambrian or Pre-Cambrian, sometimes abbreviated p?, is the largest span of time in Earth's history before the current Phanerozoic Eon, and is a Supereon divided into several eons of the geologic time scale. It spans from the formation of Earth about 4.6 billion years ago (Ga) to the beginning of the Cambrian Period, about 541 million years ago (Ma), when hard-shelled creatures first appeared in abundance. The Precambrian is so named because it precedes the Cambrian, the first period of the Phanerozoic Eon, which is named after Cambria, the classical name for Wales, where rocks from this age were first studied.

Climate

Climate is a measure of the average pattern of variation in temperature, humidity, atmospheric pressure, wind, precipitation, atmospheric particle count and other meteorological variables in a given region over long periods of time. Climate is different than weather, in that weather only describes the short-term conditions of these variables in a given region.

A region's climate is generated by the climate system, which has five components: atmosphere, hydrosphere, cryosphere, land surface, and biosphere.

Cloud

In meteorology, a cloud is a visible mass of liquid droplets or frozen crystals made of water or various chemicals suspended in the atmosphere above the surface of a planetary body. These suspended particles are also known as aerosols and are studied in the cloud physics branch of meteorology.

Terrestrial cloud formation is the result of air in Earth's atmosphere becoming saturated due to either or both of two processes; cooling of the air and adding water vapor.

Cloud cover

Cloud cover refers to the fraction of the sky obscured by clouds when observed from a particular location. Okta is the usual unit of measurement of the cloud cover. The cloud cover is correlated to the sunshine duration as the least cloudy locales are the sunniest ones while the cloudiest areas are the least sunny places.

7. Weather Systems

CHAPTER HIGHLIGHTS & NOTES: KEY TERMS, PEOPLE, PLACES, CONCEPTS

Precipitation	In meteorology, precipitation is any product of the condensation of atmospheric water vapour that falls under gravity. The main forms of precipitation include drizzle, rain, sleet, snow, graupel and hail. Precipitation occurs when a local portion of the atmosphere becomes saturated with water vapour, so that the water condenses and 'precipitates'.
Cyclone	In meteorology, a cyclone is an area of closed, circular fluid motion rotating in the same direction as the Earth. This is usually characterized by inward spiraling winds that rotate anti-clockwise in the Northern Hemisphere and clockwise in the Southern Hemisphere of the Earth. Most large-scale cyclonic circulations are centered on areas of low atmospheric pressure.
Desert	A desert is a barren area of land where little precipitation occurs and consequently living conditions are hostile for plant and animal life. The lack of vegetation exposes the unprotected surface of the ground to the processes of denudation. About one third of the land surface of the world is arid or semi-arid.
Latitude	In geography, latitude is a geographic coordinate that specifies the north-south position of a point on the Earth's surface. Latitude is an angle (defined below) which ranges from 0° at the Equator to 90° (North or South) at the poles. Lines of constant latitude, or parallels, run east-west as circles parallel to the equator.
Pressure gradient	In atmospheric sciences, the pressure gradient is a physical quantity that describes which direction and at what rate the pressure changes the most rapidly around a particular location. The pressure gradient is a dimensional quantity expressed in units of pressure per unit length, or Pa/m. Mathematically, it is obtained by applying the del operator to a pressure function of position.
Wind	Wind is the flow of gases on a large scale. On the surface of the Earth, wind consists of the bulk movement of air. In outer space, solar wind is the movement of gases or charged particles from the sun through space, while planetary wind is the outgassing of light chemical elements from a planet's atmosphere into space.
Air mass	In meteorology, an air mass is a volume of air defined by its temperature and water vapor content. Air masses cover many hundreds or thousands of square miles, and adopt the characteristics of the surface below them. They are classified according to latitude and their continental or maritime source regions.
Cold front	A cold front is defined as the leading edge of a cooler mass of air, replacing at ground level a warmer mass of air, which lies within a fairly sharp surface trough of low pressure. It forms in the wake of an extratropical cyclone, at the leading edge of its cold air advection pattern, which is also known as the cyclone's dry conveyor belt circulation. Temperature changes across the boundary can exceed 30 °C (54 °F).

Overland flow	Surface runoff (also known as overland flow) is the flow of water that occurs when excess stormwater, meltwater, or other sources flows over the earth's surface. This might occur because soil is saturated to full capacity, because rain arrives more quickly than soil can absorb it, or because impervious areas (roofs and pavement) send their runoff to surrounding soil that cannot absorb all of it. Surface runoff is a major component of the water cycle.
Dry line	A dry line is an imaginary line across a continent that separates moist air from an eastern body of water and dry desert air from the west. One of the most prominent examples of such a separation occurs in central North America, especially Texas, Oklahoma, and Kansas, where the moist air from the Gulf of Mexico meets dry air from the desert south-western states. The dry line is an important factor in severe weather frequency in the Great Plains of North America. It typically lies north-south across the High Plains states in the warm sector of an extratropical cyclone and stretches into the Canadian Prairies during the spring and early summer.
Anticyclone	An anticyclone is a weather phenomenon defined by the United States' National Weather Service's glossary as '[a] large-scale circulation of winds around a central region of high atmospheric pressure, clockwise in the Northern Hemisphere, counterclockwise in the Southern Hemisphere'. Effects of surface-based anticyclones include clearing skies as well as cooler, drier air. Fog can also form overnight within a region of higher pressure.
Trough	A 'trough' is an elongated region of relatively low atmospheric pressure, often associated with fronts. Unlike fronts, there is not a universal symbol for a trough on a weather chart. The weather charts in some countries or regions mark troughs by a line.
Tropical cyclone	A tropical cyclone is a rapidly-rotating storm system characterized by a low-pressure center, strong winds, and a spiral arrangement of thunderstorms that produce heavy rain. Tropical cyclones typically form over large bodies of relatively warm water. They derive their energy from the evaporation of water from the ocean surface, which ultimately recondenses into clouds and rain when moist air rises and cools to saturation.
Radiometric dating	Radiometric dating or radioactive dating is a technique used to date materials such as rocks or carbon, in which trace radioactive impurities were selectively incorporated when they formed. The method compares the abundance of a naturally occurring radioactive isotope within the material to the abundance of its decay products, which form at a known constant rate of decay. The use of radiometric dating was first published in 1907 by Bertram Boltwood and is now the principal source of information about the absolute age of rocks and other geological features, including the age of the Earth itself, and can be used to date a wide range of natural and man-made materials.

7. Weather Systems

CHAPTER HIGHLIGHTS & NOTES: KEY TERMS, PEOPLE, PLACES, CONCEPTS

Storm surge

A storm surge is a coastal flood or tsunami-like phenomenon of rising water commonly associated with low pressure weather systems, the severity of which is affected by the shallowness and orientation of the water body relative to storm path, and the timing of tides. Most casualties during tropical cyclones occur as the result of storm surges.

The two main meteorological factors contributing to a storm surge are a long fetch of winds spiraling inward toward the storm, and a low-pressure-induced dome of water drawn up under and trailing the storm's center.

Hurricane Katrina

Hurricane Katrina was the deadliest and most destructive Atlantic tropical cyclone of the 2005 Atlantic hurricane season. It is the costliest natural disaster, as well as one of the five deadliest hurricanes, in the history of the United States. Katrina is the seventh most intense Atlantic hurricane ever recorded, part of the 2005 season that included three of the six most intense Atlantic hurricanes ever documented (along with #1 Wilma and #4 Rita).

Thermohaline circulation

Thermohaline circulation is a part of the large-scale ocean circulation that is driven by global density gradients created by surface heat and freshwater fluxes. The adjective thermohaline derives from thermo- referring to temperature and -haline referring to salt content, factors which together determine the density of sea water. Wind-driven surface currents (such as the Gulf Stream) travel polewards from the equatorial Atlantic Ocean, cooling en route, and eventually sinking at high latitudes (forming North Atlantic Deep Water).

CHAPTER QUIZ: KEY TERMS, PEOPLE, PLACES, CONCEPTS

1. _________ is a part of the large-scale ocean circulation that is driven by global density gradients created by surface heat and freshwater fluxes. The adjective thermohaline derives from thermo- referring to temperature and -haline referring to salt content, factors which together determine the density of sea water. Wind-driven surface currents (such as the Gulf Stream) travel polewards from the equatorial Atlantic Ocean, cooling en route, and eventually sinking at high latitudes (forming North Atlantic Deep Water).

   a. New Lanark
   b. Thermohaline circulation
   c. Clear-air turbulence
   d. Climate

2. . In atmospheric sciences, the _________ is a physical quantity that describes which direction and at what rate the pressure changes the most rapidly around a particular location. The _________ is a dimensional quantity expressed in units of pressure per unit length, or Pa/m.

Mathematically, it is obtained by applying the del operator to a pressure function of position.

a. Baroclinic
b. Pressure gradient
c. Russian Empire
d. Chronometric singularity

3. In meteorology, an _________ is a volume of air defined by its temperature and water vapor content. _________es cover many hundreds or thousands of square miles, and adopt the characteristics of the surface below them. They are classified according to latitude and their continental or maritime source regions.

a. Teniente Luis Carvajal Villaroel Antarctic Base
b. West Antarctica
c. Air mass
d. British Antarctic Territory

4. A _________ is a rapidly-rotating storm system characterized by a low-pressure center, strong winds, and a spiral arrangement of thunderstorms that produce heavy rain. _________s typically form over large bodies of relatively warm water. They derive their energy from the evaporation of water from the ocean surface, which ultimately recondenses into clouds and rain when moist air rises and cools to saturation.

a. Tropical cyclone
b. Biometeorology
c. Clear-air turbulence
d. Climate

5. Surface runoff (also known as _________) is the flow of water that occurs when excess stormwater, meltwater, or other sources flows over the earth's surface. This might occur because soil is saturated to full capacity, because rain arrives more quickly than soil can absorb it, or because impervious areas (roofs and pavement) send their runoff to surrounding soil that cannot absorb all of it. Surface runoff is a major component of the water cycle.

a. Overland flow
b. West Antarctica
c. Bellingshausen Sea
d. British Antarctic Territory

ANSWER KEY
7. Weather Systems

1. b
2. b
3. c
4. a
5. a

---

8. Global Climates and Climate Change

CHAPTER OUTLINE: KEY TERMS, PEOPLE, PLACES, CONCEPTS

Streamflow

Drought

Sahel

Tropical climate

Land degradation

Positioning system

SPRING

Island

Desert

National Park

Ocean current

Sahara

Sahara Desert

Wind

Climograph

Polar climate

Climate

Paleozoic era

Arid

Equatorial climate

Boreal forest

8. Global Climates and Climate Change

CHAPTER OUTLINE: KEY TERMS, PEOPLE, PLACES, CONCEPTS

- Ice Sheet
- Mediterranean climate
- Tundra
- Antarctica
- Victoria Land
- Haifa
- Sudan
- Iran
- Sclerophyll
- Continental climate
- Boreal
- Forest
- River
- Permafrost
- Remote sensing
- Land
- Sea ice
- Seafloor spreading
- Climate change
- Precambrian
- Global climate model

8. Global Climates and Climate Change

CHAPTER OUTLINE: KEY TERMS, PEOPLE, PLACES, CONCEPTS

	Steppe
	Tropical rainforest

CHAPTER HIGHLIGHTS & NOTES: KEY TERMS, PEOPLE, PLACES, CONCEPTS

Streamflow	Streamflow, or channel runoff, is the flow of water in streams, rivers, and other channels, and is a major element of the water cycle. It is one component of the runoff of water from the land to waterbodies, the other component being surface runoff. Water flowing in channels comes from surface runoff from adjacent hillslopes, from groundwater flow out of the ground, and from water discharged from pipes.
Drought	Drought is an extended period when a region notes a deficiency in its water supply whether surface or underground water. A drought can last for months or years, or may be declared after as few as 15 days. Generally, this occurs when a region receives consistently below average precipitation.
Sahel	The Sahel[p] is the ecoclimatic and biogeographic zone of transition, in Africa, between the Sahara desert to the north and the Sudanian Savanna to the south. Having a semi-arid climate, it stretches across the southernmost extent of Northern Africa between the Atlantic Ocean and the Red Sea. The Arabic word sa?il literally means 'shore, coast', describing the appearance of the vegetation found in the Sahel as being akin to that of a coastline delimiting the sand of the Sahara.
Tropical climate	A tropical climate is a climate of the tropics. In the Köppen climate classification it is a non-arid climate in which all twelve months have mean temperatures of at least 18 °C (64 °F). Unlike the extra-tropics, where there are strong variations in day length and temperature, with season, tropical temperature remains relatively constant throughout the year and seasonal variations are dominated by precipitation.
Land degradation	Land degradation is a process in which the value of the biophysical environment is affected by combination of human-induced processes acting upon the land. also environmental degradation is the gradual destruction or reduction of the quality and quantity of human activities animals activities or natural means example water causes soil erosion, wind, etc. It is viewed as any change or disturbance to the land perceived to be deleterious or undesirable.
Positioning system	A positioning system is a mechanism for determining the location of an object in space.

Technologies for this task exist ranging from worldwide coverage with meter accuracy to workspace coverage with sub-millimetre accuracy.

SPRING

SPRING is a freeware GIS and remote sensing image processing system with an object-oriented data model which provides for the integration of raster and vector data representations in a single environment. It has Windows and Linux versions and provides a comprehensive set of functions, including tools for Satellite Image Processing, Digital Terrain Modeling, Spatial Analysis, Geostatistics, Spatial Statistics, Spatial Databases and Map Management.

SPRING is a product of Brazilian National Institute for Space Research (INPE), who is developing SPRING since 1992, and has required over 200 man/years of development and includes extensive documentation, tutorials and examples.

Island

An island or isle is any piece of sub-continental land that is surrounded by water. Very small islands such as emergent land features on atolls can be called islets, skerries, cays or keys. An island in a river or a lake island may be called an eyot or ait, or a holm.

Desert

A desert is a barren area of land where little precipitation occurs and consequently living conditions are hostile for plant and animal life. The lack of vegetation exposes the unprotected surface of the ground to the processes of denudation. About one third of the land surface of the world is arid or semi-arid.

National Park

A national park is a park in use for conservation purposes. Often it is a reserve of natural, semi-natural, or developed land that a sovereign state declares or owns. Although individual nations designate their own national parks differently, there is a common idea: the conservation of 'wild nature' for posterity and as a symbol of national pride.

Ocean current

An ocean current is a continuous, directed movement of seawater generated by the forces acting upon this mean flow, such as breaking waves, wind, Coriolis effect, cabbeling, temperature and salinity differences and tides caused by the gravitational pull of the Moon and the Sun. Depth contours, shoreline configurations and interaction with other currents influence a current's direction and strength. A deep current is any ocean current at a depth of greater than 100m.

Sahara

The Sahara is the world's hottest desert, and the third largest desert after Antarctica and the Arctic. At over 9,400,000 square kilometres (3,600,000 sq mi), it covers most of North Africa, making it almost as large as China or the United States. The Sahara stretches from the Red Sea, including parts of the Mediterranean coasts to the Atlantic Ocean.

Sahara Desert

The Sahara desert ecoregion, as defined by the World Wide Fund for Nature, includes the hyper-arid center of the Sahara, between 18° and 30° N. It is one of several desert and xeric shrubland ecoregions that cover the northern portion of the African continent.

Wind

Wind is the flow of gases on a large scale.

8. Global Climates and Climate Change

CHAPTER HIGHLIGHTS & NOTES: KEY TERMS, PEOPLE, PLACES, CONCEPTS

On the surface of the Earth, wind consists of the bulk movement of air. In outer space, solar wind is the movement of gases or charged particles from the sun through space, while planetary wind is the outgassing of light chemical elements from a planet's atmosphere into space.

Climograph

A climograph is a graphical representation of basic climatic parameters, that is monthly average temperature and precipitation, at a certain location. It is used for a quick-view of the climate of a location.

Polar climate

Regions with a polar climate are characterized by a lack of warm summers. Every month in a polar climate has an average temperature of less than 10 °C (50 °F). Regions with polar climate cover over 20% of the Earth.

Climate

Climate is a measure of the average pattern of variation in temperature, humidity, atmospheric pressure, wind, precipitation, atmospheric particle count and other meteorological variables in a given region over long periods of time. Climate is different than weather, in that weather only describes the short-term conditions of these variables in a given region.

A region's climate is generated by the climate system, which has five components: atmosphere, hydrosphere, cryosphere, land surface, and biosphere.

Paleozoic era

The Paleozoic Era (, 541 to 252.17 million years ago. It is the longest of the Phanerozoic eras, and is subdivided into six geologic periods (from oldest to youngest): the Cambrian, Ordovician, Silurian, Devonian, Carboniferous, and Permian. The Paleozoic comes after the Neoproterozoic Era of the Proterozoic Eon, and is followed by the Mesozoic Era.

The Paleozoic was a time of dramatic geological, climatic, and evolutionary change.

Arid

A region is arid when it is characterized by a severe lack of available water, to the extent of hindering or preventing the growth and development of plant and animal life. Environments subject to arid climates tend to lack vegetation and are called xeric or desertic. Most 'arid' climates surround the equator; these places include most of Africa and parts of South America, Central America and Australia.

Equatorial climate

A tropical rainforest climate, also known as an equatorial climate, is another climate name for tropical climate usually found along the equator. Regions with this climate typically feature tropical rainforests, and it is designated Af by the Köppen climate classification.

Boreal forest

Taiga also known as boreal forest or snow forest, is a biome characterized by coniferous forests consisting mostly of pines, spruces and larches.

The taiga is the world's largest terrestrial biome.

Ice Sheet	An ice sheet is a mass of glacier ice that covers surrounding terrain and is greater than 50,000 km^2, thus also known as continental glacier. The only current ice sheets are in Antarctica and Greenland; during the last glacial period at Last Glacial Maximum (LGM) the Laurentide ice sheet covered much of North America, the Weichselian ice sheet covered northern Europe and the Patagonian Ice Sheet covered southern South America. Ice sheets are bigger than ice shelves or alpine glaciers. Masses of ice covering less than 50,000 km^2 are termed an ice cap.
Mediterranean climate	A Mediterranean climate is the climate typical of the Mediterranean Basin, and is a particular variety of subtropical climate. The lands around the Mediterranean Sea form the largest area where this climate type is found, but it also prevails in much of California, in parts of Western and South Australia, in southwestern South Africa, sections of Central Asia, and in central Chile.
Tundra	In physical geography, a tundra is a biome where the tree growth is hindered by low temperatures and short growing seasons. The term tundra comes through Russian ?????? from the Kildin Sami word tundâr 'uplands', 'treeless mountain tract'. There are three types of tundra: arctic tundra, alpine tundra, and antarctic tundra.
Antarctica	Antarctica is Earth's southernmost continent, containing the geographic South Pole. It is situated in the Antarctic region of the Southern Hemisphere, almost entirely south of the Antarctic Circle, and is surrounded by the Southern Ocean. At 14.0 million km^2 (5.4 million sq mi), it is the fifth-largest continent in area after Asia, Africa, North America, and South America. For comparison, Antarctica is nearly twice the size of Australia.
Victoria Land	Victoria Land is a region of Antarctica bounded on the east by the Ross Ice Shelf and the Ross Sea and on the west by Oates Land and Wilkes Land. It was discovered by Captain James Clark Ross in January 1841 and named after the UK's Queen Victoria. The rocky promontory of Minna Bluff is often regarded as the southernmost point of Victoria Land, and separates the Scott Coast to the north from the Hillary Coast of the Ross Dependency to the south.
Haifa	Haifa is the largest city in northern Israel, and the third largest city in the country, with a population of over 272,181. Another 300,000 people live in towns directly adjacent to the city including Daliyat al-Karmel, the Krayot, Nesher, Tirat Carmel, and some Kibbuzim. Together these areas form a contiguous urban area home to nearly 600,000 residents which makes up the inner core of the Haifa metropolitan area. It is also home to the Bahá'í World Centre, a UNESCO World Heritage Site.
Sudan	The Sudan is the name given to a geographic region to the south of the Sahara, stretching from Western to eastern Central Africa. The name derives from the Arabic bilad as-sudan (???? ???????) or 'land of the Blacks' (an expression denoting West and Northern-Central Africa).

The phrase 'The Sudan' is also used to refer specifically to the modern-day country of Sudan, the western part of which forms part of the larger region, and from which South Sudan gained its independence in 2011.

Iran

Iran, also known as Persia (or), officially the Islamic Republic of Iran, is a country in Western Asia. It is bordered to the northwest by Armenia and Azerbaijan, with Kazakhstan and Russia across the Caspian Sea; to the northeast by Turkmenistan; to the east by Afghanistan and Pakistan; to the south by the Persian Gulf and the Gulf of Oman; and to the west by Turkey and Iraq. Comprising a land area of 1,648,195 km^2 (636,372 sq mi), it is the second-largest nation in the Middle East and the 18th-largest in the world; with 78.4 million inhabitants, Iran is the world's 17th most populous nation.

Sclerophyll

Sclerophyll is a type of vegetation that has hard leaves and short internodes . The word comes from the Greek sclero (hard) and phyllon (leaf).

Sclerophyllous plants occur in many parts of the world, but are most typical in the chaparral biomes.

Continental climate

Continental climate is a climate characterized by important annual variation in temperature due to the lack of significant bodies of water nearby. Often winter temperature is cold enough to support a fixed period of snow each year, and relatively moderate precipitation occurring mostly in summer, although there are exceptions such as the upper east coast areas of North America in Canada which show an even distribution of precipitation: this pattern is called Humid continental climate, but dry continental climates also exist. Regions with a continental climate exist in portions of the Northern Hemisphere continents (especially North America and Asia), and at higher elevations in other parts of the world.

Boreal

In paleoclimatology of the Holocene, the Boreal was the first of the Blytt-Sernander sequence of north European climatic phases that were originally based on the study of Danish peat bogs who first established the sequence. In peat bog sediments, the Boreal is also recognized by its characteristic pollen zone. It was preceded by the Younger Dryas, the last cold snap of the Pleistocene, and followed by the Atlantic, a warmer and moister period than our most recent climate.

Forest

A forest, also referred to as a wood or the woods, is an area with a high density of trees. As with cities, depending on various cultural definitions, what is considered a forest may vary significantly in size and have different classifications according to how and of what the forest is composed. A forest is usually an area filled with trees but any tall densely packed area of vegetation may be considered a forest, even underwater vegetation such as kelp forests, or non-vegetation such as fungi, and bacteria.

River	A river is a natural watercourse, usually freshwater, flowing towards an ocean, a lake, a sea, or another river. In a few cases, a river simply flows into the ground or dries up completely at the end of its course, and does not reach another body of water. Small rivers may be called by several other names, including stream, creek, brook, rivulet, and rill.
Permafrost	In geology, permafrost or cryotic soil is soil at or below the freezing point of water 0 °C for two or more years. Most permafrost is located in high latitudes (i.e. land close to the North and South poles), but alpine permafrost may exist at high altitudes in much lower latitudes. Ground ice is not always present, as may be in the case of nonporous bedrock, but it frequently occurs and it may be in amounts exceeding the potential hydraulic saturation of the ground material.
Remote sensing	Remote sensing is the acquisition of information about an object or phenomenon without making physical contact with the object. In modern usage, the term generally refers to the use of aerial sensor technologies to detect and classify objects on Earth (both on the surface, and in the atmosphere and oceans) by means of propagated signals (e.g. electromagnetic radiation). It may be split into active remote sensing, when a signal is first emitted from aircraft or satellites) or passive (e.g. sunlight) when information is merely recorded.
Land	Land, sometimes referred to as dry land, is the solid surface of the Earth, that is not covered by water. The division between land and ocean, sea, or other bodies of water, is one of the most fundamental separations on the planet. The vast majority of human activity has historically occurred, and continues to occur, on land.
Sea ice	Sea ice arises as seawater freezes. Because ice is less dense than water, it floats on the ocean's surface (as does fresh water ice, which has an even lower density). Sea ice covers about 7% of the Earth's surface and about 12% of the world's oceans.
Seafloor spreading	Seafloor spreading is a process that occurs at mid-ocean ridges, where new oceanic crust is formed through volcanic activity and then gradually moves away from the ridge. Seafloor spreading helps explain continental drift in the theory of plate tectonics. When oceanic plates diverge, tensional stress causes fractures to occur in the lithosphere.
Climate change	Climate change is a significant and lasting change in the statistical distribution of weather patterns over periods ranging from decades to millions of years. It may be a change in average weather conditions, or in the distribution of weather around the average conditions (i.e., more or fewer extreme weather events). Climate change is caused by factors such as biotic processes, variations in solar radiation received by Earth, plate tectonics, and volcanic eruptions.
Precambrian	The Precambrian or Pre-Cambrian, sometimes abbreviated p?, is the largest span of time in Earth's history before the current Phanerozoic Eon, and is a Supereon divided into several eons of the geologic time scale.

8. Global Climates and Climate Change

CHAPTER HIGHLIGHTS & NOTES: KEY TERMS, PEOPLE, PLACES, CONCEPTS

	It spans from the formation of Earth about 4.6 billion years ago (Ga) to the beginning of the Cambrian Period, about 541 million years ago (Ma), when hard-shelled creatures first appeared in abundance. The Precambrian is so named because it precedes the Cambrian, the first period of the Phanerozoic Eon, which is named after Cambria, the classical name for Wales, where rocks from this age were first studied.
Global climate model	A general circulation model is a mathematical model of the general circulation of a planetary atmosphere or ocean and based on the Navier-Stokes equations on a rotating sphere with thermodynamic terms for various energy sources (radiation, latent heat). These equations are the basis for complex computer programs commonly used for simulating the atmosphere or ocean of the Earth. Atmospheric and oceanic Global climate models (AGCM and OGCM) are key components of global climate models along with sea ice and land-surface components.
Steppe	In physical geography, a steppe is an ecoregion, in the montane grasslands and shrublands and temperate grasslands, savannas, and shrublands biomes, characterized by grassland plains without trees apart from those near rivers and lakes. The prairie (especially the shortgrass and mixed prairie) is an example of a steppe, though it is not usually called such. It may be semi-desert, or covered with grass or shrubs or both, depending on the season and latitude.
Tropical rainforest	A tropical rainforest is an ecosystem type that occurs roughly within the latitudes 28 degrees north or south of the equator . This ecosystem experiences high average temperatures and a significant amount of rainfall. Rainforests can be found in Asia, Australia, Africa, South America, Central America, Mexico and on many of the Pacific, Caribbean, and Indian Ocean islands.

CHAPTER QUIZ: KEY TERMS, PEOPLE, PLACES, CONCEPTS

1. An _________ is a continuous, directed movement of seawater generated by the forces acting upon this mean flow, such as breaking waves, wind, Coriolis effect, cabbeling, temperature and salinity differences and tides caused by the gravitational pull of the Moon and the Sun. Depth contours, shoreline configurations and interaction with other currents influence a current's direction and strength. A deep current is any _________ at a depth of greater than 100m.

   a. Ocean current
   b. Deep Sea Conservation Coalition
   c. Deep sea mining
   d. Vector measuring current meter

2. . _________ is a region of Antarctica bounded on the east by the Ross Ice Shelf and the Ross Sea and on the west by Oates Land and Wilkes Land. It was discovered by Captain James Clark Ross in January 1841 and named after the UK's Queen Victoria.

The rocky promontory of Minna Bluff is often regarded as the southernmost point of _________, and separates the Scott Coast to the north from the Hillary Coast of the Ross Dependency to the south.

a. Dome A
b. Herbert Range
c. Mawson Station
d. Victoria Land

3. An _________ is a mass of glacier ice that covers surrounding terrain and is greater than 50,000 km^2, thus also known as continental glacier. The only current _________s are in Antarctica and Greenland; during the last glacial period at Last Glacial Maximum (LGM) the Laurentide _________ covered much of North America, the Weichselian _________ covered northern Europe and the Patagonian _________ covered southern South America.

_________s are bigger than ice shelves or alpine glaciers. Masses of ice covering less than 50,000 km^2 are termed an ice cap.

a. Essay on the Principle of Population
b. Teniente Luis Carvajal Villaroel Antarctic Base
c. Ice Sheet
d. British Antarctic Territory

4. _________ is the largest city in northern Israel, and the third largest city in the country, with a population of over 272,181. Another 300,000 people live in towns directly adjacent to the city including Daliyat al-Karmel, the Krayot, Nesher, Tirat Carmel, and some Kibbuzim. Together these areas form a contiguous urban area home to nearly 600,000 residents which makes up the inner core of the _________ metropolitan area. It is also home to the Bahá'í World Centre, a UNESCO World Heritage Site.

a. Mughal Empire
b. Herbert Range
c. Mawson Station
d. Haifa

5. Regions with a _________ are characterized by a lack of warm summers. Every month in a _________ has an average temperature of less than 10 °C (50 °F). Regions with _________ cover over 20% of the Earth.

a. Chilling requirement
b. Polar climate
c. Climate ensemble
d. Climate of the Arctic

ANSWER KEY
8. Global Climates and Climate Change

---

1. a

2. d

3. c

4. d

5. b

---

9. Biogeographic Processes

CHAPTER OUTLINE: KEY TERMS, PEOPLE, PLACES, CONCEPTS

- Carbon cycle
- Decomposition
- Photosynthesis
- SPRING
- Soil carbon
- Biogeography
- Ecological succession
- Ecosystem
- Food chain
- Food web
- Primary producers
- Swamp
- Tropical climate
- Carbon fixation
- Chlorophyll
- Primary production
- Condensation
- Biogeochemical cycle
- Denitrification
- Nitrogen cycle
- Nitrogen fixation

9. Biogeographic Processes

CHAPTER OUTLINE: KEY TERMS, PEOPLE, PLACES, CONCEPTS

- Rhizobium
- Nitrogen
- Boreal forest
- Forest
- Sclerophyll
- Xerophyte
- Desert
- National Forest
- Fiordland
- National Park
- Habitat
- Commensalism
- Primary succession
- Protocooperation
- Secondary succession
- Autogenic succession
- Island
- Invasive species
- Remote sensing
- Speciation
- Allopatric speciation

9. Biogeographic Processes

CHAPTER OUTLINE: KEY TERMS, PEOPLE, PLACES, CONCEPTS

Genetic drift

Sympatric speciation

Endemic

Gondwana

Endangered

CHAPTER HIGHLIGHTS & NOTES: KEY TERMS, PEOPLE, PLACES, CONCEPTS

Carbon cycle

The carbon cycle is the biogeochemical cycle by which carbon is exchanged among the biosphere, pedosphere, geosphere, hydrosphere, and atmosphere of the Earth. Along with the nitrogen cycle and the water cycle, the carbon cycle comprises a sequence of events that are key to making the Earth capable of sustaining life; it describes the movement of carbon as it is recycled and reused throughout the biosphere.

The global carbon budget is the balance of the exchanges (incomes and losses) of carbon between the carbon reservoirs or between one specific loop (e.g., atmosphere ? biosphere) of the carbon cycle.

Decomposition

Decomposition is the process by which organic substances are broken down into a much simpler form of matter. The process is essential for recycling the finite matter that occupies physical space in the biome. Bodies of living organisms begin to decompose shortly after death.

Photosynthesis

Photosynthesis is a process used by plants and other organisms to convert light energy, normally from the sun, into chemical energy that can be used to fuel the organisms' activities. Carbohydrates, such as sugars, are synthesized from carbon dioxide and water (hence the name photosynthesis, from the Greek f??, phos, 'light', and s???es??, synthesis, 'putting together'). Oxygen is also released, mostly as a waste product.

SPRING

SPRING is a freeware GIS and remote sensing image processing system with an object-oriented data model which provides for the integration of raster and vector data representations in a single environment. It has Windows and Linux versions and provides a comprehensive set of functions, including tools for Satellite Image Processing, Digital Terrain Modeling, Spatial Analysis, Geostatistics, Spatial Statistics, Spatial Databases and Map Management.

9. Biogeographic Processes

CHAPTER HIGHLIGHTS & NOTES: KEY TERMS, PEOPLE, PLACES, CONCEPTS

Soil carbon	Soil carbon includes both inorganic carbon as carbonate minerals, and organic carbon as soil organic matter. Soil carbon plays a key role in the carbon cycle, and thus it is important in global climate models.
Biogeography	Biogeography is the study of the distribution of species and ecosystems in geographic space and through geological time. Organisms and biological communities vary in a highly regular fashion along geographic gradients of latitude, elevation, isolation and habitat area. Knowledge of spatial variation in the numbers and types of organisms is as vital to us today as it was to our early human ancestors, as we adapt to heterogeneous but geographically predictable environments.
Ecological succession	Ecological succession is the observed process of change in the species structure of an ecological community over time. The time scale can be decades (for example, after a wildfire), or even millions of years after a mass extinction. The community begins with relatively few pioneering plants and animals and develops through increasing complexity until it becomes stable or self-perpetuating as a climax community.
Ecosystem	An ecosystem is a community of living organisms in conjunction with the nonliving components of their environment (things like air, water and mineral soil), interacting as a system. These biotic and abiotic components are regarded as linked together through nutrient cycles and energy flows. As ecosystems are defined by the network of interactions among organisms, and between organisms and their environment, they can be of any size but usually encompass specific, limited spaces (although some scientists say that the entire planet is an ecosystem).
Food chain	A food chain is a linear network of links in a food web starting from producer organisms and ending at apex predator species (like grizzly bears or killer whales), detritivores (like earthworms or woodlice), or decomposer species (such as fungi or bacteria). A food chain also shows how the organisms are related with each other by the food they eat. Each level of a food chain represents a different trophic level.
Food web	A food web is the natural interconnection of food chains and generally a graphical representation (usually an image) of what-eats-what in an ecological community. Another name for food web is a consumer-resource system. Ecologists can broadly lump all life forms into one of two categories called trophic levels: 1) the autotrophs, and 2) the heterotrophs.
Primary producers	Primary producers are the organisms in an ecosystem that produce biomass from inorganic compounds . In almost all cases these are photosynthetically active organisms . However, there are examples of archea (unicellular organisms) that produce biomass from the oxidation of inorganic chemical compounds (chemoautotrophs) in hydrothermal vents in the deep ocean.

9. Biogeographic Processes

CHAPTER HIGHLIGHTS & NOTES: KEY TERMS, PEOPLE, PLACES, CONCEPTS

Swamp	A swamp is a wetland that is forested. Many swamps occur along large rivers where they are critically dependent upon natural water level fluctuations. Other swamps occur on the shores of large lakes.
Tropical climate	A tropical climate is a climate of the tropics. In the Köppen climate classification it is a non-arid climate in which all twelve months have mean temperatures of at least 18 °C (64 °F). Unlike the extra-tropics, where there are strong variations in day length and temperature, with season, tropical temperature remains relatively constant throughout the year and seasonal variations are dominated by precipitation.
Carbon fixation	Carbon fixation or ?arbon assimilation refers to the conversion process of inorganic carbon to organic compounds by living organisms. The most prominent example is photosynthesis, although chemosynthesis is another form of carbon fixation that can take place in the absence of sunlight. Organisms that grow by fixing carbon are called autotrophs.
Chlorophyll	Chlorophyll is a term used for several closely related green pigments found in cyanobacteria and the chloroplasts of algae and plants. Its name is derived from the Greek words ??????, chloros ('green') and f?????, phyllon ('leaf'). Chlorophyll is an extremely important biomolecule, critical in photosynthesis, which allows plants to absorb energy from light.
Primary production	In ecology, primary production is the synthesis of organic compounds from atmospheric or aqueous carbon dioxide. It principally occurs through the process of photosynthesis, which uses light as its source of energy, but it also occurs through chemosynthesis, which uses the oxidation or reduction of inorganic chemical compounds as its source of energy. Almost all life on Earth relies directly or indirectly on primary production.
Condensation	Condensation is the change of the physical state of matter from gas phase into liquid phase, and is the reverse of evaporation. The word most often refers to the water cycle. It can also be defined as the change in the state of water vapour to liquid water when in contact with a liquid or solid surface or cloud condensation nuclei within the atmosphere.
Biogeochemical cycle	In Earth science, a biogeochemical cycle or substance turnover or cycling of substances is a pathway by which a chemical substance moves through both biotic and abiotic (lithosphere, atmosphere, and hydrosphere) compartments of Earth. A cycle is a series of change which comes back to the starting point and which can be repeated. The term 'biogeochemical' tells us that biological, geological and chemical factors are all involved.
Denitrification	Denitrification is a microbially facilitated process of nitrate reduction that may ultimately produce molecular nitrogen (N_2) through a series of intermediate gaseous nitrogen oxide products. This respiratory process reduces oxidized forms of nitrogen in response to the oxidation of an electron donor such as organic matter.

Nitrogen cycle	The nitrogen cycle is the process by which nitrogen is converted between its various chemical forms. This transformation can be carried out through both biological and physical processes. Important processes in the nitrogen cycle include fixation, ammonification, nitrification, and denitrification.
Nitrogen fixation	Nitrogen fixation is a process in which nitrogen in the atmosphere is converted into ammonia (NH_3). Atmospheric nitrogen or molecular dinitrogen (N_2) is relatively inert: it does not easily react with other chemicals to form new compounds. The fixation process frees nitrogen atoms from their triply bonded diatomic form, N=N, to be used in other ways.
Rhizobium	Rhizobium is a genus of Gram-negative soil bacteria that fix nitrogen. Rhizobium forms an endosymbiotic nitrogen fixing association with roots of legumes and Parasponia. The bacteria colonize plant cells within root nodules where they convert atmospheric nitrogen into ammonia and then provide organic nitrogenous compounds such as glutamine or ureides to the plant.
Nitrogen	Nitrogen is a chemical element with symbol N and atomic number 7. It is the lightest pnictogen and at room temperature, it is a transparent, odorless diatomic gas. Nitrogen is a common element in the universe, estimated at about seventh in total abundance in the Milky Way and the Solar System. On Earth, the element forms about 78% of Earth's atmosphere and is the most abundant uncombined element.
Boreal forest	Taiga also known as boreal forest or snow forest, is a biome characterized by coniferous forests consisting mostly of pines, spruces and larches. The taiga is the world's largest terrestrial biome. In North America it covers most of inland Canada and Alaska as well as parts of the extreme northern continental United States (northern Minnesota through the Upper Peninsula of Michigan to Upstate New York and northern New England), where it is known as the Northwoods.
Forest	A forest, also referred to as a wood or the woods, is an area with a high density of trees. As with cities, depending on various cultural definitions, what is considered a forest may vary significantly in size and have different classifications according to how and of what the forest is composed. A forest is usually an area filled with trees but any tall densely packed area of vegetation may be considered a forest, even underwater vegetation such as kelp forests, or non-vegetation such as fungi, and bacteria.
Sclerophyll	Sclerophyll is a type of vegetation that has hard leaves and short internodes . The word comes from the Greek sclero (hard) and phyllon (leaf).

9. Biogeographic Processes

CHAPTER HIGHLIGHTS & NOTES: KEY TERMS, PEOPLE, PLACES, CONCEPTS

Xerophyte	A xerophyte is a species of plant that has adapted to survive in an environment with little water, such as a desert or an ice- or snow-covered region in the Alps or the Arctic. The morphology and physiology of xerophytes are variously adapted to conserve water, and commonly also to store large quantities of water, during dry periods. Other species may be adapted to survive long periods of desiccation of their tissues, during which their metabolic activity may effectively shut down.
Desert	A desert is a barren area of land where little precipitation occurs and consequently living conditions are hostile for plant and animal life. The lack of vegetation exposes the unprotected surface of the ground to the processes of denudation. About one third of the land surface of the world is arid or semi-arid.
National Forest	The National Forest is an environmental project in central England run by the National Forest Company. Portions of Leicestershire, Derbyshire and Staffordshire, 200 square miles (520 km^2) are being planted, in an attempt to blend ancient woodland with new plantings to create a new national forest. It stretches from the outskirts of Leicester in the east to Burton upon Trent in the west, and is planned link the ancient forests of Needwood and Charnwood.
Fiordland	Fiordland is a geographic region of New Zealand that is situated on the south-western corner of the South Island, comprising the western-most third of Southland. Most of Fiordland is dominated by the steep sides of the snow-capped Southern Alps, deep lakes and its ocean-flooded, steep western valleys. Indeed, the name 'Fiordland' comes from a variant spelling of the Scandinavian word for this type of steep valley, 'fjord'.
National Park	A national park is a park in use for conservation purposes. Often it is a reserve of natural, semi-natural, or developed land that a sovereign state declares or owns. Although individual nations designate their own national parks differently, there is a common idea: the conservation of 'wild nature' for posterity and as a symbol of national pride.
Habitat	A habitat is an ecological or environmental area that is inhabited by a particular species of animal, plant, or other type of organism. The term typically refers to the zone in which the organism lives and where it can find food, shelter, protection and mates for reproduction, utilizing the qualities the species has adapted to survive within the ecology of the habitat. It is the natural environment in which an organism lives, or the physical environment that surrounds a species population.
Commensalism	Commensalism, in ecology, is a class of relationships between two organisms where one organism benefits from the other without affecting it. This is in contrast with mutualism, in which both organisms benefit from each other, amensalism, where one is harmed while the other is unaffected, and parasitism, where one benefits while the other is harmed.

Primary succession	Primary succession is one of two types of biological and ecological succession of plant life, occurring in an environment in which new substrate devoid of vegetation and other organisms usually lacking soil, such as a lava flow or area left from retreated glacier, is deposited. In other words, it is the gradual growth of an ecosystem over a longer period. In contrast, secondary succession occurs on substrate that previously supported vegetation before an ecological disturbance from smaller things like floods, hurricanes, tornadoes, and fires which destroyed the plant life.
Protocooperation	Protocooperation is where two species interact with each other beneficially; they have no need to interact with each other - they interact purely for the gain that they receive from doing this. It is not at all necessary for protocooperation to occur; growth and survival is possible in the absence of the interaction. The interaction that occurs can be between different kingdoms.
Secondary succession	Secondary succession is one of the two types of ecological succession of plant life. As opposed to the first, primary succession, secondary succession is a process started by an event (e.g. forest fire, harvesting, hurricane) that reduces an already established ecosystem (e.g. a forest or a wheat field) to a smaller population of species, and as such secondary succession occurs on preexisting soil whereas primary succession usually occurs in a place lacking soil. Simply put, secondary succession is the succession that occurs after the initial succession has been disrupted and some plants and animals still exist.
Autogenic succession	In ecology, autogenic succession is succession driven by the biotic components of an ecosystem. In contrast, allogenic succession is driven by the abiotic components of the ecosystem.
Island	An island or isle is any piece of sub-continental land that is surrounded by water. Very small islands such as emergent land features on atolls can be called islets, skerries, cays or keys. An island in a river or a lake island may be called an eyot or ait, or a holm.
Invasive species	Invasive species, also called invasive exotics or simply exotics, is a nomenclature term and categorization phrase used for flora and fauna, and for specific restoration-preservation processes in native habitats, with several definitions. •The first definition, the most used, applies to introduced species that adversely affect the habitats and bioregions they invade economically, environmentally, and/or ecologically. Such invasive species may be either plants or animals and may disrupt by dominating a region, wilderness areas, particular habitats, or wildland-urban interface land from loss of natural controls (such as predators or herbivores).
Remote sensing	Remote sensing is the acquisition of information about an object or phenomenon without making physical contact with the object. In modern usage, the term generally refers to the use of aerial sensor technologies to detect and classify objects on Earth (both on the surface, and in the atmosphere and oceans) by means of propagated signals (e.g. electromagnetic radiation).

It may be split into active remote sensing, when a signal is first emitted from aircraft or satellites) or passive (e.g. sunlight) when information is merely recorded.

Speation

Speciation is the evolutionary process by which reproductively isolated biological populations evolve to become distinct species. The biologist Orator F. Cook was the first to coin the term 'speciation' for the splitting of lineages or 'cladogenesis,' as opposed to 'anagenesis' or 'phyletic evolution' occurring within lineages. Charles Darwin was the first to describe the role of natural selection in speciation.

Allopatric speciation

Allopatric speciation or geographic speciation is speciation that occurs when biological populations of the same species become vicariant, or isolated from each other to an extent that prevents or interferes with genetic interchange. This can be the result of population dispersal leading to emigration, or by geographical changes such as mountain formation, island formation, or large scale human activities (for example agricultural and civil engineering developments). The vicariant populations then undergo genotypic or phenotypic divergence as: (a) they become subjected to different selective pressures, (b) they independently undergo genetic drift, and (c) different mutations arise in the gene pools of the populations.

Genetic drift

Genetic drift is the change in the frequency of a gene variant (allele) in a population due to random sampling of organisms. The alleles in the offspring are a sample of those in the parents, and chance has a role in determining whether a given individual survives and reproduces. A population's allele frequency is the fraction of the copies of one gene that share a particular form.

Sympatric speciation

Sympatric speciation is the process through which new species evolve from a single ancestral species while inhabiting the same geographic region. In evolutionary biology and biogeography, sympatric and sympatry are terms referring to organisms whose ranges overlap or are even identical, so that they occur together at least in some places. If these organisms are closely related (e.g. sister species), such a distribution may be the result of sympatric speciation.

Endemic

Endemism is the ecological state of a species being unique to a defined geographic location, such as an island, nation, country or other defined zone, or habitat type; organisms that are indigenous to a place are not endemic to it if they are also found elsewhere. The extreme opposite of endemism is cosmopolitan distribution. Another term for a species that is endemic is precinctive, which applies to species (and subspecific categories) that are restricted to a defined geographical area.

Gondwana

In paleogeography, Gondwana, originally Gondwanaland, is the name given to the more southerly of two supercontinents which were part of the Pangaea supercontinent that existed from approximately 510 to 180 million years ago (Mya). Gondwana is believed to have sutured between ca. 570 and 510 Mya, thus joining East Gondwana to West Gondwana.

9. Biogeographic Processes

CHAPTER HIGHLIGHTS & NOTES: KEY TERMS, PEOPLE, PLACES, CONCEPTS

Endangered	An Endangered species is a species which has been categorized by the International Union for Conservation of Nature (IUCN) Red List as likely to become extinct. 'Endangered' is the second most severe conservation status for wild populations in the IUCN's schema after Critically Endangered (CR). In 2012, the IUCN Red List featured 3079 animal and 2655 plant species as Endangered worldwide.

CHAPTER QUIZ: KEY TERMS, PEOPLE, PLACES, CONCEPTS

1. _________ is the change of the physical state of matter from gas phase into liquid phase, and is the reverse of evaporation. The word most often refers to the water cycle. It can also be defined as the change in the state of water vapour to liquid water when in contact with a liquid or solid surface or cloud _________ nuclei within the atmosphere.

   a. Mughal Empire
   b. Climate Appraisal
   c. Climate ensemble
   d. Condensation

2. A _________ is a barren area of land where little precipitation occurs and consequently living conditions are hostile for plant and animal life. The lack of vegetation exposes the unprotected surface of the ground to the processes of denudation. About one third of the land surface of the world is arid or semi-arid.

   a. Biotope
   b. Blue carbon
   c. Box-Ironbark forest
   d. Desert

3. _________ are the organisms in an ecosystem that produce biomass from inorganic compounds . In almost all cases these are photosynthetically active organisms . However, there are examples of archea (unicellular organisms) that produce biomass from the oxidation of inorganic chemical compounds (chemoautotrophs) in hydrothermal vents in the deep ocean.

   a. Biotope
   b. Blue carbon
   c. Primary producers
   d. Coral reef

4. . The _________ is the biogeochemical cycle by which carbon is exchanged among the biosphere, pedosphere, geosphere, hydrosphere, and atmosphere of the Earth.

Along with the nitrogen cycle and the water cycle, the _________ comprises a sequence of events that are key to making the Earth capable of sustaining life; it describes the movement of carbon as it is recycled and reused throughout the biosphere.

The global carbon budget is the balance of the exchanges (incomes and losses) of carbon between the carbon reservoirs or between one specific loop (e.g., atmosphere ? biosphere) of the _________.

a. BBC Climate Change Experiment
b. Canadian Land Surface Scheme
c. Teniente Luis Carvajal Villaroel Antarctic Base
d. Carbon cycle

5. _________ or ?arbon assimilation refers to the conversion process of inorganic carbon to organic compounds by living organisms. The most prominent example is photosynthesis, although chemosynthesis is another form of _________ that can take place in the absence of sunlight. Organisms that grow by fixing carbon are called autotrophs.

a. Carbon fixation
b. Climate Appraisal
c. Climate ensemble
d. Climate of the Arctic

ANSWER KEY
9. Biogeographic Processes

1. d
2. d
3. c
4. d
5. a

---

10. Global Biogeography

CHAPTER OUTLINE: KEY TERMS, PEOPLE, PLACES, CONCEPTS

- Caribbean
- Fiordland
- Latin America
- National Park
- Rainforest
- Deep ocean
- Forest
- Ocean current
- Tree
- Aquatic ecosystem
- Biome
- Lichen
- Terrestrial ecosystem
- Woodland
- Climate
- Monsoon
- Evergreen forest
- National Forest
- Denali
- Coastal engineering
- Chaparral

10. Global Biogeography

CHAPTER OUTLINE: KEY TERMS, PEOPLE, PLACES, CONCEPTS

- Deforestation
- Grassland
- Savanna
- Tropical climate
- Serengeti
- Tanzania
- Steppe
- Desert
- Tundra
- Arctic tundra
- Alpine tundra
- Land cover
- Altitude
- Ecosystem
- Life zone

10. Global Biogeography

Caribbean	The Caribbean is a region that consists of the Caribbean Sea, its islands (some surrounded by the Caribbean Sea and some bordering both the Caribbean Sea and the North Atlantic Ocean), and the surrounding coasts. The region is southeast of the Gulf of Mexico and the North American mainland, east of Central America, and north of South America. Situated largely on the Caribbean Plate, the region comprises more than 700 islands, islets, reefs, and cays.
Fiordland	Fiordland is a geographic region of New Zealand that is situated on the south-western corner of the South Island, comprising the western-most third of Southland. Most of Fiordland is dominated by the steep sides of the snow-capped Southern Alps, deep lakes and its ocean-flooded, steep western valleys. Indeed, the name 'Fiordland' comes from a variant spelling of the Scandinavian word for this type of steep valley, 'fjord'.
Latin America	Latin America is the subregion of the Americas comprising those countries where Romance languages are spoken, primarily Spanish and Portuguese. It consists of twenty sovereign states which cover an area that stretches from the southern border of the United States to the southern tip of South America, including the Caribbean. Latin America has an area of approximately 19,197,000 km^2 (7,412,000 sq mi), almost 13% of the earth's land surface area.
National Park	A national park is a park in use for conservation purposes. Often it is a reserve of natural, semi-natural, or developed land that a sovereign state declares or owns. Although individual nations designate their own national parks differently, there is a common idea: the conservation of 'wild nature' for posterity and as a symbol of national pride.
Rainforest	Rainforests are forests characterized by high rainfall, with annual rainfall between 250 centimetres to 450 centimetres (180 in). The monsoon trough, alternatively known as the intertropical convergence zone, plays a significant role in creating the climatic conditions necessary for the Earth's tropical rainforests. Around 40% to 75% of all biotic species are indigenous to the rainforests.
Deep ocean	The deep sea or deep layer is the lowest layer in the ocean, existing below the thermocline and above the seabed, at a depth of 1000 fathoms or more. Little or no light penetrates this part of the ocean, and most of the organisms that live there rely for subsistence on falling organic matter produced in the photic zone. For this reason, scientists once assumed that life would be sparse in the deep ocean, but virtually every probe has revealed that, on the contrary, life is abundant in the deep ocean.
Forest	A forest, also referred to as a wood or the woods, is an area with a high density of trees. As with cities, depending on various cultural definitions, what is considered a forest may vary significantly in size and have different classifications according to how and of what the forest is composed.

10. Global Biogeography

CHAPTER HIGHLIGHTS & NOTES: KEY TERMS, PEOPLE, PLACES, CONCEPTS

Ocean current	An ocean current is a continuous, directed movement of seawater generated by the forces acting upon this mean flow, such as breaking waves, wind, Coriolis effect, cabbeling, temperature and salinity differences and tides caused by the gravitational pull of the Moon and the Sun. Depth contours, shoreline configurations and interaction with other currents influence a current's direction and strength. A deep current is any ocean current at a depth of greater than 100m.
Tree	In botany, a tree is a perennial plant with an elongated stem, or trunk, supporting leaves or branches. In some usages, the definition of a tree may be narrower, including only woody plants, only plants that are usable as lumber or only plants above a specified height. At its broadest, trees include the taller palms, the tree ferns, bananas and bamboo.
Aquatic ecosystem	An aquatic ecosystem is an ecosystem in a body of water. Communities of organisms that are dependent on each other and on their environment live in aquatic ecosystems. The two main types of aquatic ecosystems are marine ecosystems and freshwater ecosystems.
Biome	Biomes are climatically and geographically defined as contiguous areas with similar climatic conditions on the Earth, such as communities of plants, animals, and soil organisms, and are often referred to as ecosystems. Some parts of the earth have more or less the same kind of abiotic and biotic factors spread over a large area, creating a typical ecosystem over that area. Such major ecosystems are termed as biomes.
Lichen	A lichen is a composite organism consisting of a fungus (the mycobiont) and a photosynthetic partner (the photobiont or phycobiont) growing together in a symbiotic relationship. The photobiont is usually either a green alga (commonly Trebouxia) or cyanobacterium (commonly Nostoc). The morphology, physiology and biochemistry of lichens are very different from those of the isolated fungus and alga in culture.
Terrestrial ecosystem	A terrestrial ecosystem is an ecosystem found only on landforms. Six primary terrestrial ecosystems exist: tundra, taiga, temperate deciduous forest, tropical rain forest, grassland and desert. A community of organisms and their environment that occurs on the land masses of continents and islands.
Woodland	Woodland is a low-density forest forming open habitats with plenty of sunlight and limited shade. Woodlands may support an understory of shrubs and herbaceous plants including grasses. Woodland may form a transition to shrubland under drier conditions or during early stages of primary or secondary succession.

10. Global Biogeography

CHAPTER HIGHLIGHTS & NOTES: KEY TERMS, PEOPLE, PLACES, CONCEPTS

Climate	Climate is a measure of the average pattern of variation in temperature, humidity, atmospheric pressure, wind, precipitation, atmospheric particle count and other meteorological variables in a given region over long periods of time. Climate is different than weather, in that weather only describes the short-term conditions of these variables in a given region. A region's climate is generated by the climate system, which has five components: atmosphere, hydrosphere, cryosphere, land surface, and biosphere.
Monsoon	Monsoon is traditionally defined as a seasonal reversing wind accompanied by corresponding changes in precipitation, but is now used to describe seasonal changes in atmospheric circulation and precipitation associated with the asymmetric heating of land and sea. Usually, the term monsoon is used to refer to the rainy phase of a seasonally-changing pattern, although technically there is also a dry phase. The major monsoon systems of the world consist of the West African and Asia-Australian monsoons.
Evergreen forest	An evergreen forest is a forest consisting entirely or mainly of evergreen trees that retain green foliage all year round. Such forests reign the tropics primarily as broadleaf evergreens, and in temperate and boreal latitudes primarily as coniferous evergreens. Moist forest, montane forest,mossy forests, Laurel forest, cloud forest, fog forest, are generally tropical or subtropical or mild temperate evergreen forest, found in areas with high humidity and relatively stable and mild temperatures, characterized by a persistent, frequent or seasonal low-level cloud cover, usually at the canopy level.
National Forest	The National Forest is an environmental project in central England run by the National Forest Company. Portions of Leicestershire, Derbyshire and Staffordshire, 200 square miles (520 km^2) are being planted, in an attempt to blend ancient woodland with new plantings to create a new national forest. It stretches from the outskirts of Leicester in the east to Burton upon Trent in the west, and is planned link the ancient forests of Needwood and Charnwood.
Denali	Denali is the highest mountain peak in North America, with a summit elevation of 20,310 feet (6,190 m) above sea level. At some 18,000 ft (5,500 m), the base-to-peak rise is the largest of any mountain situated entirely above sea level. With a topographic prominence of 20,156 feet (6,144 m) and a topographic isolation of 4,629 miles (7,450 km), Denali is the third most prominent and third most isolated peak after Mount Everest and Aconcagua.
Coastal engineering	Coastal engineering is the branch of civil engineering concerning the specific demands posed by constructing at or near the coast, as well as the development of the coast itself.

10. Global Biogeography

The hydrodynamic impact of especially waves, tides, storm surges and tsunamis and the harsh environment of salt seawater are typical challenges for the coastal engineer - as are the morphodynamic changes of the coastal topography, caused both by the autonomous development of the system and man-made changes. The areas of interest in coastal engineering include the coasts of the oceans, seas, marginal seas, estuaries and big lakes.

Chaparral

Chaparral is a shrubland or heathland plant community found primarily in the U.S. state of California and in the northern portion of the Baja California peninsula, Mexico. It is shaped by a Mediterranean climate (mild, wet winters and hot dry summers) and wildfire, featuring summer-drought tolerant plants with hard sclerophyllous evergreen leaves, as contrasted with the associated soft-leaved, drought deciduous, scrub community of Coastal sage scrub, found below the chaparral biome. Chaparral covers 5% of the state of California, and associated Mediterranean shrubland an additional 3.5%.

Deforestation

Deforestation, clearance or clearing is the removal of a forest or stand of trees where the land is thereafter converted to a non-forest use. Examples of deforestation include conversion of forestland to farms, ranches, or urban use.

More than half of the animal and plant species in the world live in tropical forests.

Grassland

Grasslands are areas where the vegetation is dominated by grasses, however sedge (Cyperaceae) and rush (Juncaceae) families can also be found. Grasslands occur naturally on all continents except Antarctica. Grasslands are found in most ecoregions of the Earth. For example there are five terrestrial ecoregion classifications (subdivisions) of the temperate grasslands, savannas, and shrublands biome ('ecosystem'), which is one of eight terrestrial ecozones of the Earth's surface.

Savanna

It is often believed that savannas feature widely spaced, scattered trees. However, in many savannas, tree densities are higher and trees are more regularly spaced than in forest. Savannas are also characterized by seasonal water availability, with the majority of rainfall confined to one season.

Tropical climate

A tropical climate is a climate of the tropics. In the Köppen climate classification it is a non-arid climate in which all twelve months have mean temperatures of at least 18 °C (64 °F). Unlike the extra-tropics, where there are strong variations in day length and temperature, with season, tropical temperature remains relatively constant throughout the year and seasonal variations are dominated by precipitation.

Serengeti

The Serengeti ecosystem is a geographical region in Africa. It is located in north Tanzania and extends to south-western Kenya between latitudes 1 and 3 degrees south latitude and 34 and 36 degrees east longitude. It spans some 30,000 km^2 (12,000 sq mi).

10. Global Biogeography

Tanzania	Tanzania, officially the United Republic of Tanzania, is a country in East Africa in the African Great Lakes region. It is bordered by Kenya and Uganda to the north; Rwanda, Burundi, and the Democratic Republic of the Congo to the west; and Zambia, Malawi, and Mozambique to the south. The country's eastern border is formed by the Indian Ocean.
Steppe	In physical geography, a steppe is an ecoregion, in the montane grasslands and shrublands and temperate grasslands, savannas, and shrublands biomes, characterized by grassland plains without trees apart from those near rivers and lakes. The prairie (especially the shortgrass and mixed prairie) is an example of a steppe, though it is not usually called such. It may be semi-desert, or covered with grass or shrubs or both, depending on the season and latitude.
Desert	A desert is a barren area of land where little precipitation occurs and consequently living conditions are hostile for plant and animal life. The lack of vegetation exposes the unprotected surface of the ground to the processes of denudation. About one third of the land surface of the world is arid or semi-arid.
Tundra	In physical geography, a tundra is a biome where the tree growth is hindered by low temperatures and short growing seasons. The term tundra comes through Russian ?????? from the Kildin Sami word tundâr 'uplands', 'treeless mountain tract'. There are three types of tundra: arctic tundra, alpine tundra, and antarctic tundra.
Arctic tundra	In physical geography, tundra is a type of biome where the tree growth is hindered by low temperatures and short growing seasons. The term tundra comes through Russian ?????? (tûndra) from the Kildin Sami word tundâr 'uplands', 'treeless mountain tract'. There are three types of tundra: arctic tundra, alpine tundra, and Antarctic tundra.
Alpine tundra	Alpine tundra is a type of natural region or biome that does not contain trees because it is at high altitude. Alpine tundra is distinguished from arctic tundra, because alpine soils are generally better drained than arctic soils. Alpine tundra transitions to subalpine forests below the tree line; stunted forests occurring at the forest-tundra ecotone are known as Krummholz.
Land cover	Land cover is the physical material at the surface of the earth. Land covers include grass, asphalt, trees, bare ground, water, etc. There are two primary methods for capturing information on land cover: field survey and analysis of remotely sensed imagery.
Altitude	Altitude or height is defined based on the context in which it is used . As a general definition, altitude is a distance measurement, usually in the vertical or 'up' direction, between a reference datum and a point or object. The reference datum also often varies according to the context.
Ecosystem	An ecosystem is a community of living organisms in conjunction with the nonliving components of their environment (things like air, water and mineral soil), interacting as a system. These biotic and abiotic components are regarded as linked together through nutrient cycles and energy flows.

10. Global Biogeography

CHAPTER HIGHLIGHTS & NOTES: KEY TERMS, PEOPLE, PLACES, CONCEPTS

Life zone	The Life Zone concept was developed by C. Hart Merriam in 1889 as a means of describing areas with similar plant and animal communities. Merriam observed that the changes in these communities with an increase in latitude at a constant elevation are similar to the changes seen with an increase in elevation at a constant latitude. The life zones Merriam identified are most applicable to western North America, being developed on the San Francisco Peaks, Arizona and Cascade Range of the northwestern USA. He tried to develop a system that is applicable across the North American continent, but that system is rarely referred to.

CHAPTER QUIZ: KEY TERMS, PEOPLE, PLACES, CONCEPTS

1. In physical geography, a _________ is a biome where the tree growth is hindered by low temperatures and short growing seasons. The term _________ comes through Russian ?????? from the Kildin Sami word tundâr 'uplands', 'treeless mountain tract'. There are three types of _________: arctic _________, alpine _________, and antarctic _________.

   a. Mangrove
   b. Tundra
   c. Mediterranean forests, woodlands, and scrub
   d. Mire

2. An _________ is a continuous, directed movement of seawater generated by the forces acting upon this mean flow, such as breaking waves, wind, Coriolis effect, cabbeling, temperature and salinity differences and tides caused by the gravitational pull of the Moon and the Sun. Depth contours, shoreline configurations and interaction with other currents influence a current's direction and strength. A deep current is any _________ at a depth of greater than 100m.

   a. Beach nourishment
   b. Deep Sea Conservation Coalition
   c. Deep sea mining
   d. Ocean current

3. . In physical geography, tundra is a type of biome where the tree growth is hindered by low temperatures and short growing seasons. The term tundra comes through Russian ?????? (tûndra) from the Kildin Sami word tundâr 'uplands', 'treeless mountain tract'. There are three types of tundra: _________, alpine tundra, and Ant_________.

   a. Arctic tundra
   b. Maritime coast range ponderosa pine forest
   c. Mediterranean forests, woodlands, and scrub

4. The _________ concept was developed by C. Hart Merriam in 1889 as a means of describing areas with similar plant and animal communities. Merriam observed that the changes in these communities with an increase in latitude at a constant elevation are similar to the changes seen with an increase in elevation at a constant latitude.

   The _________s Merriam identified are most applicable to western North America, being developed on the San Francisco Peaks, Arizona and Cascade Range of the northwestern USA. He tried to develop a system that is applicable across the North American continent, but that system is rarely referred to.

   a. Teniente Luis Carvajal Villaroel Antarctic Base
   b. Cattle drive
   c. Diel vertical migration
   d. Life zone

5. The _________ ecosystem is a geographical region in Africa. It is located in north Tanzania and extends to south-western Kenya between latitudes 1 and 3 degrees south latitude and 34 and 36 degrees east longitude. It spans some 30,000 km^2 (12,000 sq mi). The Kenyan part of the _________ is known as Maasai (Masai) Mara.

   a. Serengeti
   b. Kaokoveld
   c. Lake Natron
   d. Mandara Plateau mosaic

ANSWER KEY
10. Global Biogeography

---

1. b
2. d
3. a
4. d
5. a

You can take the complete Online Interactive Chapter Practice Test

for 10. Global Biogeography
on all key terms, persons, places, and concepts.

No Additional Costs

http://www.Cram101.com

Register, send an email request to Travis.Reese@Cram101.com to get your user Id and password.

Include your customer order number, and ISBN number from your studyguide Retailer.

11. Global Soils

CHAPTER OUTLINE: KEY TERMS, PEOPLE, PLACES, CONCEPTS

- Climate change
- Biogeography
- Land
- Organic matter
- Parent material
- Soil texture
- Weathering
- Horizon
- Soil formation
- Soil structure
- Mineral alteration
- Wilting point
- Climate
- Evapotranspiration
- Eluviation
- Calcification
- Salinization
- Coastline
- SPRING
- Antarctica
- Victoria Land

11. Global Soils

CHAPTER OUTLINE: KEY TERMS, PEOPLE, PLACES, CONCEPTS

Histosol

CHAPTER HIGHLIGHTS & NOTES: KEY TERMS, PEOPLE, PLACES, CONCEPTS

Climate change	Climate change is a significant and lasting change in the statistical distribution of weather patterns over periods ranging from decades to millions of years. It may be a change in average weather conditions, or in the distribution of weather around the average conditions (i.e., more or fewer extreme weather events). Climate change is caused by factors such as biotic processes, variations in solar radiation received by Earth, plate tectonics, and volcanic eruptions.
Biogeography	Biogeography is the study of the distribution of species and ecosystems in geographic space and through geological time. Organisms and biological communities vary in a highly regular fashion along geographic gradients of latitude, elevation, isolation and habitat area. Knowledge of spatial variation in the numbers and types of organisms is as vital to us today as it was to our early human ancestors, as we adapt to heterogeneous but geographically predictable environments.
Land	Land, sometimes referred to as dry land, is the solid surface of the Earth, that is not covered by water. The division between land and ocean, sea, or other bodies of water, is one of the most fundamental separations on the planet. The vast majority of human activity has historically occurred, and continues to occur, on land.
Organic matter	Organic matter or organic material, natural organic matter, NOM is matter composed of organic compounds that has come from the remains of organisms such as plants and animals and their waste products in the environment. Organic molecules can also be made by chemical reactions that don't involve life. Basic structures are created from cellulose, tannin, cutin, and lignin, along with other various proteins, lipids, and carbohydrates.
Parent material	Parent material is the underlying geological material in which soil horizons form. Soils typically inherit a great deal of structure and minerals from their parent material, and, as such, are often classified based upon their contents of consolidated or unconsolidated mineral material that has undergone some degree of physical or chemical weathering and the mode by which the materials were most recently transported.
Soil texture	Soil texture is known as a qualitative classification instruments used both the field and laboratory for agricultural soils to determine classes for based on their physical texture.

while classes are distinguished in the field and the class is then used to determine crop suitability and to approximate the soils responses to environmental and management conditions such as drought or calcium (lime) requirements. A qualitative rather than a quantitative tool it is a fast, simple and effective means to assess a soil's physical characteristics.

Weathering

Weathering is the breaking down of rocks, soil and minerals as well as artificial materials through contact with the Earth's atmosphere, biota and waters. Weathering occurs in situ, roughly translated to: 'with no movement', and thus should not be confused with erosion, which involves the movement of rocks and minerals by agents such as water, ice, snow, wind, waves and gravity and then being transported and deposited in other locations.

Two important classifications of weathering processes exist - physical and chemical weathering; each sometimes involves a biological component.

Horizon

The horizon is the apparent line that separates earth from sky, the line that divides all visible directions into two categories: those that intersect the Earth's surface, and those that do not. At many locations, the true horizon is obscured by trees, buildings, mountains, etc., and the resulting intersection of earth and sky is called the visible horizon. When looking at a sea from a shore, the part of the sea closest to the horizon is called the offing.

Soil formation

Pedogenesis (also termed soil development, soil evolution, soil formation, and soil genesis) is the process of soil formation as regulated by the effects of place, environment, and history. Biogeochemical processes act to both create and destroy order (anisotropy) within soils. These alterations lead to the development of layers, termed soil horizons, distinguished by differences in color, structure, texture, and chemistry.

Soil structure

Soil structure describes the arrangement of the solid parts of the soil and of the pore space located between them. It is determined by how individual soil granules clump or bind together and aggregate, and therefore, the arrangement of soil pores between them. Soil structure has a major influence on water and air movement, biological activity, root growth and seedling emergence.

Mineral alteration

Mineral alteration refers to the various natural processes that alter a mineral's chemical composition or crystallography.

Mineral alteration is essentially governed by the laws of thermodynamics related to energy conservation, relevant to environmental conditions, often in presence of catalysts, the most common and influential being water .

The degree and scales of time in which different minerals alter vary depending on the initial product and its physical properties and susceptibility to alteration.

Wilting point

Permanent wilting point is defined as the minimal point of soil moisture the plant requires not to wilt.

If moisture decreases to this or any lower point a plant wilts and can no longer recover its turgidity when placed in a saturated atmosphere for 12 hours. The physical definition of the wilting point is defined as the water content at -1500 J/kg (or -15 bar) of suction pressure, or negative hydraulic head.

Climate

Climate is a measure of the average pattern of variation in temperature, humidity, atmospheric pressure, wind, precipitation, atmospheric particle count and other meteorological variables in a given region over long periods of time. Climate is different than weather, in that weather only describes the short-term conditions of these variables in a given region.

A region's climate is generated by the climate system, which has five components: atmosphere, hydrosphere, cryosphere, land surface, and biosphere.

Evapotranspiration

Evapotranspiration is the sum of evaporation and plant transpiration from the Earth's land surface to atmosphere. Evaporation accounts for the movement of water to the air from sources such as the soil, canopy interception, and waterbodies. Transpiration accounts for the movement of water within a plant and the subsequent loss of water as vapor through stomata in its leaves.

Eluviation

In geology, eluvium or eluvial deposits are those geological deposits and soils that are derived by in situ weathering or weathering plus gravitational movement or accumulation.

The process of removal of materials from geological or soil horizons is called eluviation or leaching. There is a difference in the usage of this term in geology and soil science.

Calcification

Calcification is the accumulation of calcium salts in a body tissue. It normally occurs in the formation of bone, but calcium can be deposited abnormally in soft tissue, causing it to harden. Calcifications may be classified on whether there is mineral balance or not, and the location of the calcification.

Salinization

Soil salinity is the salt content in the soil; the process of increasing the salt content is known as salinization. Salts occur naturally within soils and water. Salination can be caused by natural processes such as mineral weathering or by the gradual withdrawal of an ocean.

Coastline

A coastline or a seashore is the area where land meets the sea or ocean, or a line that forms the boundary between the land and the ocean or a lake. A precise line that can be called a coastline cannot be determined due to the Coastline paradox.

The term coastal zone is a region where interaction of the sea and land processes occurs.

SPRING

SPRING is a freeware GIS and remote sensing image processing system with an object-oriented data model which provides for the integration of raster and vector data representations in a single environment.

11. Global Soils

CHAPTER HIGHLIGHTS & NOTES: KEY TERMS, PEOPLE, PLACES, CONCEPTS

It has Windows and Linux versions and provides a comprehensive set of functions, including tools for Satellite Image Processing, Digital Terrain Modeling, Spatial Analysis, Geostatistics, Spatial Statistics, Spatial Databases and Map Management.

SPRING is a product of Brazilian National Institute for Space Research (INPE), who is developing SPRING since 1992, and has required over 200 man/years of development and includes extensive documentation, tutorials and examples.

Antarctica

Antarctica is Earth's southernmost continent, containing the geographic South Pole. It is situated in the Antarctic region of the Southern Hemisphere, almost entirely south of the Antarctic Circle, and is surrounded by the Southern Ocean. At 14.0 million km^2 (5.4 million sq mi), it is the fifth-largest continent in area after Asia, Africa, North America, and South America. For comparison, Antarctica is nearly twice the size of Australia.

Victoria Land

Victoria Land is a region of Antarctica bounded on the east by the Ross Ice Shelf and the Ross Sea and on the west by Oates Land and Wilkes Land. It was discovered by Captain James Clark Ross in January 1841 and named after the UK's Queen Victoria. The rocky promontory of Minna Bluff is often regarded as the southernmost point of Victoria Land, and separates the Scott Coast to the north from the Hillary Coast of the Ross Dependency to the south.

Histosol

In both the FAO soil classification and the USDA soil taxonomy, a histosol is a soil consisting primarily of organic materials. They are defined as having 40 centimetres (16 in) or more of organic soil material in the upper 80 centimetres (31 in). Organic soil material has an organic carbon content (by weight) of 12 to 18 percent, or more, depending on the clay content of the soil.

CHAPTER QUIZ: KEY TERMS, PEOPLE, PLACES, CONCEPTS

1. _________ or organic material, natural _________, NOM is matter composed of organic compounds that has come from the remains of organisms such as plants and animals and their waste products in the environment. Organic molecules can also be made by chemical reactions that don't involve life. Basic structures are created from cellulose, tannin, cutin, and lignin, along with other various proteins, lipids, and carbohydrates.

a. Essay on the Principle of Population
b. Organic matter
c. British Society for Geomorphology
d. Catena

2. . _________ refers to the various natural processes that alter a mineral's chemical composition or crystallography.

_________ is essentially governed by the laws of thermodynamics related to energy conservation, relevant to environmental conditions, often in presence of catalysts, the most common and influential being water .

The degree and scales of time in which different minerals alter vary depending on the initial product and its physical properties and susceptibility to alteration.

a. Mughal Empire
b. Seral
c. Russian Empire
d. Mineral alteration

3. _________ is a significant and lasting change in the statistical distribution of weather patterns over periods ranging from decades to millions of years. It may be a change in average weather conditions, or in the distribution of weather around the average conditions (i.e., more or fewer extreme weather events). _________ is caused by factors such as biotic processes, variations in solar radiation received by Earth, plate tectonics, and volcanic eruptions.

a. Teniente Luis Carvajal Villaroel Antarctic Base
b. West Antarctica
c. Climate change
d. British Antarctic Territory

4. In both the FAO soil classification and the USDA soil taxonomy, a _________ is a soil consisting primarily of organic materials. They are defined as having 40 centimetres (16 in) or more of organic soil material in the upper 80 centimetres (31 in). Organic soil material has an organic carbon content (by weight) of 12 to 18 percent, or more, depending on the clay content of the soil.

a. Histosol
b. Herbert Range
c. Mawson Station
d. Mount Breckinridge

5. Soil salinity is the salt content in the soil; the process of increasing the salt content is known as _________. Salts occur naturally within soils and water. Salination can be caused by natural processes such as mineral weathering or by the gradual withdrawal of an ocean.

a. Salinization
b. Mughal Empire
c. Russian Empire
d. Climate classification

ANSWER KEY
11. Global Soils

---

1. b
2. d
3. c
4. a
5. a

---

12. Earth Materials and Plate Tectonics

CHAPTER OUTLINE: KEY TERMS, PEOPLE, PLACES, CONCEPTS

- Precambrian
- Cenozoic era
- Mesozoic era
- Paleozoic era
- Uniformitarianism
- Radiometric dating
- Asthenosphere
- Continental crust
- Lithosphere
- Island
- Oceanic crust
- Lava
- Magma
- National Park
- Fault scarp
- Ultramafic rock
- Sediment
- Serengeti
- SPRING
- Tanzania
- Peat

12. Earth Materials and Plate Tectonics

CHAPTER OUTLINE: KEY TERMS, PEOPLE, PLACES, CONCEPTS

- Marble
- Quartzite
- Schist
- North Pole
- Topography
- Humidity
- Shuttle Radar Topography Mission
- Great Basin
- Deccan Plateau
- Tarim Basin
- Seafloor spreading
- Ocean
- Atlantic
- Continental drift
- Pangea
- Rodinia
- Continental margin
- Island arc
- Red Sea
- Soil formation
- Radiogenic

12. Earth Materials and Plate Tectonics

CHAPTER OUTLINE: KEY TERMS, PEOPLE, PLACES, CONCEPTS

Tectonic

CHAPTER HIGHLIGHTS & NOTES: KEY TERMS, PEOPLE, PLACES, CONCEPTS

Precambrian

The Precambrian or Pre-Cambrian, sometimes abbreviated p?, is the largest span of time in Earth's history before the current Phanerozoic Eon, and is a Supereon divided into several eons of the geologic time scale. It spans from the formation of Earth about 4.6 billion years ago (Ga) to the beginning of the Cambrian Period, about 541 million years ago (Ma), when hard-shelled creatures first appeared in abundance. The Precambrian is so named because it precedes the Cambrian, the first period of the Phanerozoic Eon, which is named after Cambria, the classical name for Wales, where rocks from this age were first studied.

Cenozoic era

The Cenozoic Era is the current and most recent of the three Phanerozoic geological eras, following the Mesozoic Era and covering the period from 66 million years ago to present day.

The Cenozoic is also known as the Age of Mammals, because the extinction of many groups allowed mammals to greatly diversify.

Early in the Cenozoic, following the K-Pg event, the planet was dominated by relatively small fauna, including small mammals, birds, reptiles, and amphibians.

Mesozoic era

The Mesozoic Era is an interval of geological time from about 252 to 66 million years ago. It is also called the Age of Reptiles, a phrase introduced by the 19th century paleontologist Gideon Mantell who viewed it as dominated by reptiles such as Iguanodon, Megalosaurus, Plesiosaurus and what are now called Pseudosuchia.

Mesozoic means 'middle life', deriving from the Greek prefix meso-/μes?- for 'between' and zoon/???? meaning 'animal' or 'living being'.

Paleozoic era

The Paleozoic Era (, 541 to 252.17 million years ago. It is the longest of the Phanerozoic eras, and is subdivided into six geologic periods (from oldest to youngest): the Cambrian, Ordovician, Silurian, Devonian, Carboniferous, and Permian. The Paleozoic comes after the Neoproterozoic Era of the Proterozoic Eon, and is followed by the Mesozoic Era.

The Paleozoic was a time of dramatic geological, climatic, and evolutionary change.

Uniformitarianism	Uniformitarianism was an assumption that the same natural laws and processes that operate in the universe now have always operated in the universe in the past and apply everywhere in the universe. It has included the gradualistic concept that 'the present is the key to the past' and is functioning at the same rates. Uniformitarianism has been a key first principle of geology and virtually all fields of science, but naturalism's modern geologists, while accepting that geology has occurred across deep time, no longer hold to a strict gradualism.
Radiometric dating	Radiometric dating or radioactive dating is a technique used to date materials such as rocks or carbon, in which trace radioactive impurities were selectively incorporated when they formed. The method compares the abundance of a naturally occurring radioactive isotope within the material to the abundance of its decay products, which form at a known constant rate of decay. The use of radiometric dating was first published in 1907 by Bertram Boltwood and is now the principal source of information about the absolute age of rocks and other geological features, including the age of the Earth itself, and can be used to date a wide range of natural and man-made materials.
Asthenosphere	The asthenosphere is the highly viscous, mechanically weak and ductilely deforming region of the upper mantle of the Earth. It lies below the lithosphere, at depths between approximately 80 and 200 km (50 and 120 miles) below the surface. The Lithosphere-Asthenosphere boundary is usually referred to as LAB. The asthenosphere is generally solid, although some of its regions could be melted (e.g., below mid-ocean ridges).
Continental crust	The continental crust is the layer of igneous, sedimentary, and metamorphic rocks that forms the continents and the areas of shallow seabed close to their shores, known as continental shelves. This layer is sometimes called sial because its bulk composition is more felsic compared to the oceanic crust, called sima which has a more mafic bulk composition. Changes in seismic wave velocities have shown that at a certain depth (the Conrad discontinuity), there is a reasonably sharp contrast between the more felsic upper continental crust and the lower continental crust, which is more mafic in character.
Lithosphere	The lithosphere is the rigid outermost shell of a rocky planet defined on the basis of the mechanical properties. On Earth, it comprises the crust and the portion of the upper mantle that behaves elastically on time scales of thousands of years or greater. The outermost shell of a rocky planet defined on the basis of the chemistry and mineralogy is a crust.
Island	An island or isle is any piece of sub-continental land that is surrounded by water. Very small islands such as emergent land features on atolls can be called islets, skerries, cays or keys. An island in a river or a lake island may be called an eyot or ait, or a holm.
Oceanic crust	Oceanic crust is the uppermost layer of the oceanic portion of a tectonic plate. The crust overlies the solidified and uppermost layer of the mantle. The crust and the solid mantle layer together comprise oceanic lithosphere.

12. Earth Materials and Plate Tectonics

CHAPTER HIGHLIGHTS & NOTES: KEY TERMS, PEOPLE, PLACES, CONCEPTS

Lava	Lava is the molten rock expelled by a volcano during an eruption. The resulting rock after solidification and cooling is also called lava. The molten rock is formed in the interior of some planets, including Earth, and some of their satellites.
Magma	Magma is a mixture of molten or semi-molten rock, volatiles and solids that is found beneath the surface of the Earth, and is expected to exist on other terrestrial planets and some natural satellites. Besides molten rock, magma may also contain suspended crystals, dissolved gas and sometimes gas bubbles. Magma often collects in magma chambers that may feed a volcano or solidify underground to form an intrusion.
National Park	A national park is a park in use for conservation purposes. Often it is a reserve of natural, semi-natural, or developed land that a sovereign state declares or owns. Although individual nations designate their own national parks differently, there is a common idea: the conservation of 'wild nature' for posterity and as a symbol of national pride.
Fault scarp	A fault scarp is a small step or offset on the ground surface where one side of a fault has moved vertically with respect to the other. It is the topographic expression of faulting attributed to the displacement of the land surface by movement along faults. They are exhibited either by differential movement and subsequent erosion along an old inactive geologic fault (a sort of old rupture), or by a movement on a recent active fault.
Ultramafic rock	Ultramafic are igneous and meta-igneous rocks with a very low silica content (less than 45%), generally >18% MgO, high FeO, low potassium, and are composed of usually greater than 90% mafic minerals (dark colored, high magnesium and iron content). The Earth's mantle is composed of ultramafic rocks. Ultrabasic is a more inclusive term that includes igneous rocks with low silica content that may not be extremely enriched in Fe and Mg, such as carbonatites and ultrapotassic igneous rocks.
Sediment	Sediment is a naturally occurring material that is broken down by processes of weathering and erosion, and is subsequently transported by the action of wind, water, or ice, and/or by the force of gravity acting on the particles. For example, silt falls out of suspension via sedimentation and forms soil (some of which may eventually become sedimentary rock). Sediments are most often transported by water (fluvial processes), wind (aeolian processes) and glaciers.
Serengeti	The Serengeti ecosystem is a geographical region in Africa. It is located in north Tanzania and extends to south-western Kenya between latitudes 1 and 3 degrees south latitude and 34 and 36 degrees east longitude. It spans some 30,000 km^2 (12,000 sq mi). The Kenyan part of the Serengeti is known as Maasai (Masai) Mara.

SPRING	SPRING is a freeware GIS and remote sensing image processing system with an object-oriented data model which provides for the integration of raster and vector data representations in a single environment. It has Windows and Linux versions and provides a comprehensive set of functions, including tools for Satellite Image Processing, Digital Terrain Modeling, Spatial Analysis, Geostatistics, Spatial Statistics, Spatial Databases and Map Management. SPRING is a product of Brazilian National Institute for Space Research (INPE), who is developing SPRING since 1992, and has required over 200 man/years of development and includes extensive documentation, tutorials and examples.
Tanzania	Tanzania, officially the United Republic of Tanzania, is a country in East Africa in the African Great Lakes region. It is bordered by Kenya and Uganda to the north; Rwanda, Burundi, and the Democratic Republic of the Congo to the west; and Zambia, Malawi, and Mozambique to the south. The country's eastern border is formed by the Indian Ocean.
Peat	Peat is an accumulation of partially decayed vegetation or organic matter that is unique to natural areas called peatlands, bogs, or mires. The peatland ecosystem is the most efficient carbon sink on the planet because peatland plants capture the CO_2 which is naturally released from the peat, thus maintaining an equilibrium. In natural peatlands, the 'annual rate of biomass production is greater than the rate of decomposition', but it takes 'thousands of years for peatlands to develop the deposits of 1.5 to 2.3 m, which is the average depth of the boreal peatlands'.
Marble	Marble is a virtual globe that allows the user to choose among the Earth, the Moon, Venus, Mars and other planets. It is free software under the terms of the GNU LGPL, developed by KDE for use on personal computers and smart phones. It is written in C++ and uses Qt 4.
Quartzite	Quartzite is a hard, non-foliated metamorphic rock which was originally pure quartz sandstone. Sandstone is converted into quartzite through heating and pressure usually related to tectonic compression within orogenic belts. Pure quartzite is usually white to grey, though quartzites often occur in various shades of pink and red due to varying amounts of iron oxide (Fe_2O_3).
Schist	Schist is a medium-grade metamorphic rock with medium to large, flat, sheet-like grains in a preferred orientation (nearby grains are roughly parallel). It is defined by having more than 50% platy and elongated minerals, often finely interleaved with quartz and feldspar. These lamellar (flat, planar) minerals include micas, chlorite, talc, hornblende, graphite, and others.
North Pole	The North Pole, also known as the Geographic North Pole or Terrestrial North Pole, is defined as the point in the Northern Hemisphere where the Earth's axis of rotation meets its surface. It should not be confused with the North Magnetic Pole. The North Pole is the northernmost point on the Earth, lying diametrically opposite the South Pole.

12. Earth Materials and Plate Tectonics

CHAPTER HIGHLIGHTS & NOTES: KEY TERMS, PEOPLE, PLACES, CONCEPTS

Topography	Topography is a field of planetary science comprising the study of surface shape and features of the Earth and other observable astronomical objects including planets, moons, and asteroids. It is also the description of such surface shapes and features (especially their depiction in maps). The topography of an area could also mean the surface shape and features themselves.
Humidity	Humidity is the amount of water vapor in the air. Water vapor is the gaseous state of water and is invisible. Humidity indicates the likelihood of precipitation, dew, or fog.
Shuttle Radar Topography Mission	The Shuttle Radar Topography Mission is an international research effort that obtained digital elevation models on a near-global scale from 56° S to 60° N, to generate the most complete high-resolution digital topographic database of Earth prior to the release of the ASTER GDEM in 2009. Shuttle Radar Topography Mission consisted of a specially modified radar system that flew on board the Space Shuttle Endeavour during the 11-day STS-99 mission in February 2000, based on the older Spaceborne Imaging Radar-C/X-band Synthetic Aperture Radar (SIR-C/X-SAR), previously used on the Shuttle in 1994. To acquire topographic (elevation) data, the Shuttle Radar Topography Mission payload was outfitted with two radar antennas. One antenna was located in the Shuttle's payload bay, the other - a critical change from the SIR-C/X-SAR, allowing single-pass interferometry - on the end of a 60-meter (200-foot) mast that extended from the payload bay once the Shuttle was in space. The technique employed is known as Interferometric Synthetic Aperture Radar.
Great Basin	The Great Basin is the largest area of contiguous endorheic watersheds in North America. It is noted for both its arid climate and the Basin and range topography that varies from the North American low point at Badwater Basin to the highest point of the contiguous United States, less than 100 miles (160 km) away at the summit of Mount Whitney. The region spans several physiographic divisions, biomes/ecoregions, and deserts.
Deccan Plateau	The Deccan Plateau is a large plateau in India, making up most of the southern part of the country. It rises a hundred metres high in the north, and more than a kilometre high in the south, forming a raised triangle within the familiar downward-pointing triangle of the Indian subcontinent's coastline. It extends over eight Indian states and encompasses a wide range of habitats, covering most of central and southern India.
Tarim Basin	The Tarim Basin is a large endorheic basin in northwest China occupying an area of about 906,500 km^2 . Located in China's Xinjiang region, it is sometimes used metonymously for the southern half of the province, or Nanjiang (Turkish: tarim havzasi, Chinese: ??; pinyin: Nánjiang; literally 'Southern Xinjiang'). Its northern boundary is the Tian Shan mountain range and its southern boundary is the Kunlun Mountains on the edge of the Qinghai-Tibet Plateau.
Seafloor spreading	Seafloor spreading is a process that occurs at mid-ocean ridges, where new oceanic crust is formed through volcanic activity and then gradually moves away from the ridge.

Seafloor spreading helps explain continental drift in the theory of plate tectonics. When oceanic plates diverge, tensional stress causes fractures to occur in the lithosphere.

Ocean

An ocean is a body of saline water that composes much of a planet's hydrosphere. On Earth, an ocean is one or all of the major divisions of the planet's World Ocean - which are, in descending order of area, the Pacific, Atlantic, Indian, Southern (Antarctic), and Arctic Oceans. The word sea is often used interchangeably with 'ocean' in American English but, strictly speaking, a sea is a body of saline water (generally a division of the World Ocean) that land partly or fully encloses.

Atlantic

The Atlantic in palaeoclimatology was the warmest and moistest Blytt-Sernander period, pollen zone and chronozone of Holocene northern Europe. The climate was generally warmer than today. It was preceded by the Boreal, with a climate similar to today's, and was followed by the Subboreal, a transition to the modern.

Continental drift

Continental drift is the movement of the Earth's continents relative to each other, thus appearing to 'drift' across the ocean bed. The speculation that continents might have 'drifted' was first put forward by Abraham Ortelius in 1596. The concept was independently and more fully developed by Alfred Wegener in 1912, but his theory was rejected by some for lack of a mechanism (though this was supplied later by Arthur Holmes) and others because of prior theoretical commitments. The idea of continental drift has been subsumed by the theory of plate tectonics, which explains how the continents move.

Pangea

Pangaea or Pangea was a supercontinent that existed during the late Paleozoic and early Mesozoic eras. It assembled from earlier continental units approximately 300 million years ago, and it began to break apart about 175 million years ago. In contrast to the present Earth and its distribution of continental mass, much of Pangaea was in the southern hemisphere and surrounded by a super ocean, Panthalassa.

Rodinia

Rodinia is a Neoproterozoic supercontinent that was assembled 1.3-0.9 billion years ago and broke up 750-600 million years ago. Valentine & Moores 1970 were probably the first to recognise a Precambrian supercontinent, which they named 'Pangaea I'. It was renamed 'Rodinia' by McMenamin & McMenamin 1990 who also were the first to produce a reconstruction and propose a temporal framework for the supercontinent.

Continental margin

The continental margin is the zone of the ocean floor that separates the thin oceanic crust from thick continental crust. Together, the continental shelf, continental slope, and continental rise are called continental margin. Continental margins constitute about 28% of the oceanic area.

Island arc

An island arc is a type of archipelago, often composed of a chain of volcanoes, with arc-shaped alignment, situated parallel and close to a boundary between two converging tectonic plates.

Most of these island arcs are formed as one oceanic tectonic plate subducts another one and, in most cases, produces magma at depth below the over-riding plate. However, this is only true for those island arcs that are part of the group of mountain belts which are called volcanic arcs, a term which is used when all the elements of the arc-shaped mountain belt are composed of volcanoes.

Red Sea

The Red Sea is a seawater inlet of the Indian Ocean, lying between Africa and Asia. The connection to the ocean is in the south through the Bab el Mandeb strait and the Gulf of Aden. In the north, there is the Sinai Peninsula, the Gulf of Aqaba, and the Gulf of Suez (leading to the Suez Canal).

Soil formation

Pedogenesis (also termed soil development, soil evolution, soil formation, and soil genesis) is the process of soil formation as regulated by the effects of place, environment, and history. Biogeochemical processes act to both create and destroy order (anisotropy) within soils. These alterations lead to the development of layers, termed soil horizons, distinguished by differences in color, structure, texture, and chemistry.

Radiogenic

A radiogenic nuclide is a nuclide that is produced by a process of radioactive decay. It may itself be radioactive (a radionuclide) or stable (a stable nuclide).

Radiogenic nuclides (more commonly referred to as radiogenic isotopes) form some of the most important tools in geology.

Tectonic

Tectonics (from the Late Latin tectonicus from the Greek te?t??????, 'pertaining to building') is concerned with the processes which control the structure and properties of the Earth's crust, and its evolution through time. In particular, it describes the processes of mountain building, the growth and behavior of the strong, old cores of continents known as cratons, and the ways in which the relatively rigid plates that comprise the Earth's outer shell interact with each other. Tectonics also provides a framework to understand the earthquake and volcanic belts which directly affect much of the global population.

1. _________ is an accumulation of partially decayed vegetation or organic matter that is unique to natural areas called peatlands, bogs, or mires. The peatland ecosystem is the most efficient carbon sink on the planet because peatland plants capture the CO_2 which is naturally released from the _________, thus maintaining an equilibrium. In natural peatlands, the 'annual rate of biomass production is greater than the rate of decomposition', but it takes 'thousands of years for peatlands to develop the deposits of 1.5 to 2.3 m, which is the average depth of the boreal peatlands'.

   a. Mughal Empire
   b. Peat
   c. CityEngine
   d. Commercial Joint Mapping Toolkit

2. A _________ is a small step or offset on the ground surface where one side of a fault has moved vertically with respect to the other. It is the topographic expression of faulting attributed to the displacement of the land surface by movement along faults. They are exhibited either by differential movement and subsequent erosion along an old inactive geologic fault (a sort of old rupture), or by a movement on a recent active fault.

   a. Mughal Empire
   b. Russian Empire
   c. Fault scarp
   d. Sohm Abyssal Plain

3. The _________ is a seawater inlet of the Indian Ocean, lying between Africa and Asia. The connection to the ocean is in the south through the Bab el Mandeb strait and the Gulf of Aden. In the north, there is the Sinai Peninsula, the Gulf of Aqaba, and the Gulf of Suez (leading to the Suez Canal).

   a. Red Sea
   b. Cocos Island
   c. Mediterranean Sea
   d. Rothera Research Station

4. A _________ nuclide is a nuclide that is produced by a process of radioactive decay. It may itself be radioactive (a radionuclide) or stable (a stable nuclide).

   _________ nuclides (more commonly referred to as _________ isotopes) form some of the most important tools in geology.

   a. Radiogenic
   b. Seral
   c. Russian Empire
   d. Rothera Research Station

5. . _________ or radioactive dating is a technique used to date materials such as rocks or carbon, in which trace radioactive impurities were selectively incorporated when they formed. The method compares the abundance of a naturally occurring radioactive isotope within the material to the abundance of its decay products, which form at a known constant rate of decay.

12. Earth Materials and Plate Tectonics

CHAPTER QUIZ: KEY TERMS, PEOPLE, PLACES, CONCEPTS

The use of _________ was first published in 1907 by Bertram Boltwood and is now the principal source of information about the absolute age of rocks and other geological features, including the age of the Earth itself, and can be used to date a wide range of natural and man-made materials.

a. Mughal Empire
b. Cenozoic
c. Radiometric dating
d. Paleozoic

ANSWER KEY
12. Earth Materials and Plate Tectonics

1. b
2. c
3. a
4. a
5. c

You can take the complete Online Interactive Chapter Practice Test

for 12. Earth Materials and Plate Tectonics
on all key terms, persons, places, and concepts.

No Additional Costs

http://www.Cram101.com

13. Tectonic and Volcanic Landforms

CHAPTER OUTLINE: KEY TERMS, PEOPLE, PLACES, CONCEPTS

- Tectonic
- Mesozoic era
- Fault scarp
- Graben
- Hebgen Lake
- Lake
- Epicenter
- Richter scale
- Secondary succession
- Mexico City earthquake
- Tsunami
- Environment
- Iran
- Magma
- Temperature record
- Sonoran Desert
- Remote sensing
- Shuttle Radar Topography Mission
- Erosion
- Island
- Caldera

13. Tectonic and Volcanic Landforms

CHAPTER OUTLINE: KEY TERMS, PEOPLE, PLACES, CONCEPTS

	Geothermal

CHAPTER HIGHLIGHTS & NOTES: KEY TERMS, PEOPLE, PLACES, CONCEPTS

Tectonic	Tectonics (from the Late Latin tectonicus from the Greek te?t??????, 'pertaining to building') is concerned with the processes which control the structure and properties of the Earth's crust, and its evolution through time. In particular, it describes the processes of mountain building, the growth and behavior of the strong, old cores of continents known as cratons, and the ways in which the relatively rigid plates that comprise the Earth's outer shell interact with each other. Tectonics also provides a framework to understand the earthquake and volcanic belts which directly affect much of the global population.
Mesozoic era	The Mesozoic Era is an interval of geological time from about 252 to 66 million years ago. It is also called the Age of Reptiles, a phrase introduced by the 19th century paleontologist Gideon Mantell who viewed it as dominated by reptiles such as Iguanodon, Megalosaurus, Plesiosaurus and what are now called Pseudosuchia. Mesozoic means 'middle life', deriving from the Greek prefix meso-/μes?- for 'between' and zoon/???? meaning 'animal' or 'living being'.
Fault scarp	A fault scarp is a small step or offset on the ground surface where one side of a fault has moved vertically with respect to the other. It is the topographic expression of faulting attributed to the displacement of the land surface by movement along faults. They are exhibited either by differential movement and subsequent erosion along an old inactive geologic fault (a sort of old rupture), or by a movement on a recent active fault.
Graben	In geology, a graben is a depressed block of land bordered by parallel faults. Graben is German for ditch or trench. The plural form is either grabens.
Hebgen Lake	Hebgen Lake is a lake located in Southwest Montana and is created by Hebgen Dam. It is well known for a magnitude 7.1 to 7.5 earthquake which occurred nearby on August 17, 1959, forming Quake Lake which is located immediately downstream.
Lake	A lake is a body of relatively still water of considerable size, localized in a basin, that is surrounded by land apart from a river, stream, or other form of moving water that serves to feed or drain the lake. Lakes are inland and not part of the ocean and therefore are distinct from lagoons, and are larger and deeper than ponds.

Epicenter

The epicenter, epicentre / or epicentrum is the point on the Earth's surface that is directly above the hypocentre or focus, the point where an earthquake or underground explosion originates. The word derives from the New Latin noun epicentrum, the latinisation of the ancient Greek adjective ?p??e?t??? (epikentros), 'occupying a cardinal point, situated on a centre', from ?p? (epi) 'on, upon, at' and ???t??? (kentron) 'centre'. The term was coined by the Irish seismologist Robert Mallet.

The word, however, is frequently misused to mean 'center', such that 'center' is now one dictionary definition of the term.

Richter scale

The Richter magnitude scale (also Richter scale) assigns a magnitude number to quantify the energy released by an earthquake. The Richter scale, developed in the 1930s, is a base-10 logarithmic scale, which defines magnitude as the logarithm of the ratio of the amplitude of the seismic waves to an arbitrary, minor amplitude.

As measured with a seismometer, an earthquake that registers 5.0 on the Richter scale has a shaking amplitude 10 times that of an earthquake that registered 4.0, and thus corresponds to a release of energy 31.6 times that released by the lesser earthquake.

Secondary succession

Secondary succession is one of the two types of ecological succession of plant life. As opposed to the first, primary succession, secondary succession is a process started by an event (e.g. forest fire, harvesting, hurricane) that reduces an already established ecosystem (e.g. a forest or a wheat field) to a smaller population of species, and as such secondary succession occurs on preexisting soil whereas primary succession usually occurs in a place lacking soil.

Simply put, secondary succession is the succession that occurs after the initial succession has been disrupted and some plants and animals still exist.

Mexico City earthquake

The 1985 Mexico City earthquake was a magnitude 8.1 earthquake that struck some states of Mexico and Mexico City on the early morning of 19 September 1985 at around 7:19 am, caused the deaths of at least 10,000 people and serious damage to the Greater Mexico City Area. The complete seismic event consisted of four quakes. A pre-event quake of magnitude 5.2 occurred on 28 May 1985. The main and most powerful shock occurred 19 September, followed by two aftershocks: one on 20 September 1985 of magnitude 7.5 and the fourth occurring seven months later on 30 April 1986 of magnitude 7.0. The quakes were located off the Mexican Pacific coast, more than 350 kilometres (220 mi) away, but due to strength of the quake and the fact that Mexico City sits on an old lakebed, Mexico City suffered major damage.

Tsunami

A tsunami also known as a seismic sea wave, is a series of waves in a water body caused by the displacement of a large volume of water, generally in an ocean or a large lake.

13. Tectonic and Volcanic Landforms

CHAPTER HIGHLIGHTS & NOTES: KEY TERMS, PEOPLE, PLACES, CONCEPTS

Environment — The biophysical environment is the biotic and abiotic surrounding of an organism or population, and includes the factors that have an influence in their survival, development and evolution. The term environment can refer to different concepts, but is often used as a short form for the biophysical environment. This practice is common, for instance, among governments which entitle agencies dealing with the biophysical environment with denominations such as Environment agency.

Iran — Iran, also known as Persia (or), officially the Islamic Republic of Iran, is a country in Western Asia. It is bordered to the northwest by Armenia and Azerbaijan, with Kazakhstan and Russia across the Caspian Sea; to the northeast by Turkmenistan; to the east by Afghanistan and Pakistan; to the south by the Persian Gulf and the Gulf of Oman; and to the west by Turkey and Iraq. Comprising a land area of 1,648,195 km^2 (636,372 sq mi), it is the second-largest nation in the Middle East and the 18th-largest in the world; with 78.4 million inhabitants, Iran is the world's 17th most populous nation.

Magma — Magma is a mixture of molten or semi-molten rock, volatiles and solids that is found beneath the surface of the Earth, and is expected to exist on other terrestrial planets and some natural satellites. Besides molten rock, magma may also contain suspended crystals, dissolved gas and sometimes gas bubbles. Magma often collects in magma chambers that may feed a volcano or solidify underground to form an intrusion.

Temperature record — The temperature record shows the fluctuations of the temperature of the atmosphere and the oceans through various spans of time. The most detailed information exists since 1850, when methodical thermometer-based records began. There are numerous estimates of temperatures since the end of the Pleistocene glaciation, particularly during the current Holocene epoch.

Sonoran Desert — The Sonoran Desert is a North American desert which covers large parts of the Southwestern United States in Arizona and California, and of Northwestern Mexico in Sonora, Baja California and Baja California Sur. It is one of the largest and hottest deserts in North America, with an area of 311,000 square kilometers (120,000 sq mi). The western portion of the United States-Mexico border passes through the Sonoran Desert.

Remote sensing — Remote sensing is the acquisition of information about an object or phenomenon without making physical contact with the object. In modern usage, the term generally refers to the use of aerial sensor technologies to detect and classify objects on Earth (both on the surface, and in the atmosphere and oceans) by means of propagated signals (e.g. electromagnetic radiation). It may be split into active remote sensing, when a signal is first emitted from aircraft or satellites) or passive (e.g. sunlight) when information is merely recorded.

Shuttle Radar Topography Mission — The Shuttle Radar Topography Mission is an international research effort that obtained digital elevation models on a near-global scale from 56° S to 60° N, to generate the most complete high-resolution digital topographic database of Earth prior to the release of the ASTER GDEM in 2009.

Shuttle Radar Topography Mission consisted of a specially modified radar system that flew on board the Space Shuttle Endeavour during the 11-day STS-99 mission in February 2000, based on the older Spaceborne Imaging Radar-C/X-band Synthetic Aperture Radar (SIR-C/X-SAR), previously used on the Shuttle in 1994. To acquire topographic (elevation) data, the Shuttle Radar Topography Mission payload was outfitted with two radar antennas. One antenna was located in the Shuttle's payload bay, the other - a critical change from the SIR-C/X-SAR, allowing single-pass interferometry - on the end of a 60-meter (200-foot) mast that extended from the payload bay once the Shuttle was in space. The technique employed is known as Interferometric Synthetic Aperture Radar.

Erosion

In earth science, erosion is the action of surface processes that remove soil, rock, or dissolved material from one location on the Earth's crust, then transport it away to another location. The particulate breakdown of rock or soil into clastic sediment is referred to as physical or mechanical erosion; this contrasts with chemical erosion, where soil or rock material is removed from an area by its dissolving into a solvent (typically water), followed by the flow away of that solution. Eroded sediment or solutes may be transported just a few millimetres, or for thousands of kilometres.

Island

An island or isle is any piece of sub-continental land that is surrounded by water. Very small islands such as emergent land features on atolls can be called islets, skerries, cays or keys. An island in a river or a lake island may be called an eyot or ait, or a holm.

Caldera

A caldera is a large cauldron-like volcanic depression, a type of volcanic crater, formed by the collapse of an emptied magma chamber. The depression often originates in very big explosive eruptions. The emptying of this magma chamber may be also be accomplished more gradually by a series of effusive eruptions from the volcanic system, even kilometers away from the magma chamber itself.

Geothermal

Geothermal gradient is the rate of increasing temperature with respect to increasing depth in the Earth's interior. Away from tectonic plate boundaries, it is about 25 °C per km of depth (1 °F per 70 feet of depth) near the surface in most of the world. Strictly speaking, geo-thermal necessarily refers to the Earth but the concept may be applied to other planets.

13. Tectonic and Volcanic Landforms

CHAPTER QUIZ: KEY TERMS, PEOPLE, PLACES, CONCEPTS

1. _________s (from the Late Latin tectonicus from the Greek te?t??????, 'pertaining to building') is concerned with the processes which control the structure and properties of the Earth's crust, and its evolution through time. In particular, it describes the processes of mountain building, the growth and behavior of the strong, old cores of continents known as cratons, and the ways in which the relatively rigid plates that comprise the Earth's outer shell interact with each other. _________s also provides a framework to understand the earthquake and volcanic belts which directly affect much of the global population.

   a. Mughal Empire
   b. Russian Empire
   c. Tectonic
   d. Basilica of Our Lady of Peace

2. _________ is a lake located in Southwest Montana and is created by Hebgen Dam. It is well known for a magnitude 7.1 to 7.5 earthquake which occurred nearby on August 17, 1959, forming Quake Lake which is located immediately downstream.

   a. Hebgen Lake
   b. Gallatin Range
   c. Teniente Luis Carvajal Villaroel Antarctic Base
   d. Guinean Forests of West Africa

3. _________ gradient is the rate of increasing temperature with respect to increasing depth in the Earth's interior. Away from tectonic plate boundaries, it is about 25 °C per km of depth (1 °F per 70 feet of depth) near the surface in most of the world. Strictly speaking, geo-thermal necessarily refers to the Earth but the concept may be applied to other planets.

   a. Mughal Empire
   b. Geothermal
   c. Sigsbee Deep
   d. Sohm Abyssal Plain

4. The _________ is an interval of geological time from about 252 to 66 million years ago. It is also called the Age of Reptiles, a phrase introduced by the 19th century paleontologist Gideon Mantell who viewed it as dominated by reptiles such as Iguanodon, Megalosaurus, Plesiosaurus and what are now called Pseudosuchia.

   Mesozoic means 'middle life', deriving from the Greek prefix meso-/μes?- for 'between' and zoon/???? meaning 'animal' or 'living being'.

   a. Paleozoic era
   b. Cenozoic era
   c. Mesozoic era
   d. Mesozoic

5. . The _________, epicentre / or epicentrum is the point on the Earth's surface that is directly above the hypocentre or focus, the point where an earthquake or underground explosion originates.

The word derives from the New Latin noun epicentrum, the latinisation of the ancient Greek adjective ?p??e?t??? (epikentros), 'occupying a cardinal point, situated on a centre', from ?p? (epi) 'on, upon, at' and ???t??? (kentron) 'centre'. The term was coined by the Irish seismologist Robert Mallet.

The word, however, is frequently misused to mean 'center', such that 'center' is now one dictionary definition of the term.

a. Epicenter
b. Body of water
c. Bourne
d. Brine pool

ANSWER KEY
13. Tectonic and Volcanic Landforms

---

1. c
2. a
3. b
4. c
5. a

---

14. Weathering and Mass Wasting

CHAPTER OUTLINE: KEY TERMS, PEOPLE, PLACES, CONCEPTS

- Mass balance
- Chemical weathering
- Denudation
- Erosion
- Regolith
- Capillary action
- Carbonic acid
- Oxidation
- Bedrock
- Sediment
- Mass wasting
- Soil creep
- Solifluction
- Scree
- Lake
- Scarification
- Strip mining
- Remote sensing

14. Weathering and Mass Wasting

CHAPTER HIGHLIGHTS & NOTES: KEY TERMS, PEOPLE, PLACES, CONCEPTS

Mass balance	A mass balance, also called a material balance, is an application of conservation of mass to the analysis of physical systems. By accounting for material entering and leaving a system, mass flows can be identified which might have been unknown, or difficult to measure without this technique. The exact conservation law used in the analysis of the system depends on the context of the problem, but all revolve around mass conservation, i.e. that matter cannot disappear or be created spontaneously.
Chemical weathering	Weathering is the breaking down of rocks, soil and minerals as well as artificial materials through contact with the Earth's atmosphere, biota and waters. Weathering occurs in situ, roughly translated to: 'with no movement', and thus should not be confused with erosion, which involves the movement of rocks and minerals by agents such as water, ice, snow, wind, waves and gravity and then being transported and deposited in other locations. Two important classifications of weathering processes exist - physical and chemical weathering; each sometimes involves a biological component.
Denudation	In geology, denudation is the long-term sum of processes that cause the wearing away of the Earth's surface by moving water, ice, wind and waves, leading to a reduction in elevation and relief of landforms and landscapes. Endogenous processes such as volcanoes, earthquakes, and plate tectonics uplift and expose continental crust to the exogenous processes of weathering, erosion, and mass wasting.
Erosion	In earth science, erosion is the action of surface processes that remove soil, rock, or dissolved material from one location on the Earth's crust, then transport it away to another location. The particulate breakdown of rock or soil into clastic sediment is referred to as physical or mechanical erosion; this contrasts with chemical erosion, where soil or rock material is removed from an area by its dissolving into a solvent (typically water), followed by the flow away of that solution. Eroded sediment or solutes may be transported just a few millimetres, or for thousands of kilometres.
Regolith	Regolith is a layer of loose, heterogeneous superficial material covering solid rock. It includes dust, soil, broken rock, and other related materials and is present on Earth, the Moon, Mars, some asteroids, and other terrestrial planets and moons.
Capillary action	Capillary action is the ability of a liquid to flow in narrow spaces without the assistance of, or even in opposition to, external forces like gravity. The effect can be seen in the drawing up of liquids between the hairs of a paint-brush, in a thin tube, in porous materials such as paper and plaster, in some non-porous materials such as sand and liquefied carbon fiber, or in a cell. It occurs because of intermolecular forces between the liquid and surrounding solid surfaces.
Carbonic acid	Carbonic acid is a chemical compound with the chemical formula H_2CO_3 (equivalently OC_2). It is also a name sometimes given to solutions of carbon dioxide in water (carbonated water), because such solutions contain small amounts of H_2CO_3.

Oxidation	Redox is a contraction of the name for a chemical reduction-oxidation reaction. A reduction reaction always occurs with an oxidation reaction. Redox reactions include all chemical reactions in which atoms have their oxidation state changed; in general, redox reactions involve the transfer of electrons between chemical species.
Bedrock	In geology, bedrock is the lithified rock that lies under the loose softer material at the surface of the Earth or other terrestrial planet. The broken and weathered regolith includes soil and subsoil. The surface of the bedrock beneath soil cover is known as rockhead in engineering geology and its identification by digging, drilling or geophysical methods is an important task in most civil engineering projects.
Sediment	Sediment is a naturally occurring material that is broken down by processes of weathering and erosion, and is subsequently transported by the action of wind, water, or ice, and/or by the force of gravity acting on the particles. For example, silt falls out of suspension via sedimentation and forms soil (some of which may eventually become sedimentary rock). Sediments are most often transported by water (fluvial processes), wind (aeolian processes) and glaciers.
Mass wasting	Mass wasting, also known as slope movement or mass movement, is the geomorphic process by which soil, sand, regolith, and rock move downslope typically as a mass, largely under the force of gravity, but frequently affected by water and water content as in submarine environments and mudflows. Types of mass wasting include creep, slides, flows, topples, and falls, each with its own characteristic features, and taking place over timescales from seconds to years. Mass wasting occurs on both terrestrial and submarine slopes, and has been observed on Earth, Mars, Venus, and Jupiter's moon Io.
Soil creep	Downhill creep, also known as soil creep or commonly just creep, is the slow downward progression of rock and soil down a low grade slope; it can also refer to slow deformation of such materials as a result of prolonged pressure and stress. Creep may appear to an observer to be continuous, but it really is the sum of numerous minute, discrete movements of slope material caused by the force of gravity. Friction, being the primary force to resist gravity, is produced when one body of material slides past another offering a mechanical resistance between the two which acts to hold objects (or slopes) in place.
Solifluction	In geomorphology, solifluction is a gradual mass wasting slope process related to freeze-thaw activity, occurring in periglacial environments. In 1906 Johan Gunnar Andersson interpreted solifluction as a mass wasting process that occurs most commonly in colder climates where periods of freezing and thawing are regular occurrences. A type of creep process, solifluction describes the slow downslope movement of water-saturated sediment due to recurrent freezing and thawing of the ground, affected by gravity.

14. Weathering and Mass Wasting

CHAPTER HIGHLIGHTS & NOTES: KEY TERMS, PEOPLE, PLACES, CONCEPTS

Scree	Scree is a collection of broken rock fragments at the base of crags, mountain cliffs, volcanoes or valley shoulders that has accumulated through periodic rockfall from adjacent cliff faces. Landforms associated with these materials are often called talus deposits. Talus deposits typically have a concave upwards form, while the maximum inclination corresponds to the angle of repose of the mean debris size.
Lake	A lake is a body of relatively still water of considerable size, localized in a basin, that is surrounded by land apart from a river, stream, or other form of moving water that serves to feed or drain the lake. Lakes are inland and not part of the ocean and therefore are distinct from lagoons, and are larger and deeper than ponds. Lakes can be contrasted with rivers or streams, which are usually flowing.
Scarification	Scarifying (also scarification modification) involves scratching, etching, burning / branding, or superficially cutting designs, pictures, or words into the skin as a permanent body modification. In the process of body scarification, scars are formed by cutting or branding the skin by varying methods (sometimes using further sequential aggravating wound healing methods at timed intervals, like irritation), to purposely influence wound healing to scar more and not scar less. Scarification is sometimes called cicatrization (from the French equivalent).
Strip mining	Surface mining, including strip mining, open-pit mining and mountaintop removal mining, is a broad category of mining in which soil and rock overlying the mineral deposit are removed. In contrast to underground mining, in which the overlying rock is left in place, and the mineral removed through shafts or tunnels. Surface mining began in the mid-sixteenth century and is practiced throughout the world, although the majority of surface mining occurs in North America. It gained popularity throughout the 20th century, and is now the predominant form of mining in coal beds such as those in Appalachia and America's Midwest.
Remote sensing	Remote sensing is the acquisition of information about an object or phenomenon without making physical contact with the object. In modern usage, the term generally refers to the use of aerial sensor technologies to detect and classify objects on Earth (both on the surface, and in the atmosphere and oceans) by means of propagated signals (e.g. electromagnetic radiation). It may be split into active remote sensing, when a signal is first emitted from aircraft or satellites) or passive (e.g. sunlight) when information is merely recorded.

1. A _________, also called a material balance, is an application of conservation of mass to the analysis of physical systems. By accounting for material entering and leaving a system, mass flows can be identified which might have been unknown, or difficult to measure without this technique. The exact conservation law used in the analysis of the system depends on the context of the problem, but all revolve around mass conservation, i.e. that matter cannot disappear or be created spontaneously.

   a. Mughal Empire
   b. Mass balance
   c. Survival International
   d. Basilica of Our Lady of Peace

2. Weathering is the breaking down of rocks, soil and minerals as well as artificial materials through contact with the Earth's atmosphere, biota and waters. Weathering occurs in situ, roughly translated to: 'with no movement', and thus should not be confused with erosion, which involves the movement of rocks and minerals by agents such as water, ice, snow, wind, waves and gravity and then being transported and deposited in other locations.

   Two important classifications of weathering processes exist - physical and _________; each sometimes involves a biological component.

   a. Chemical weathering
   b. Mughal Empire
   c. Russian Empire
   d. Survival International

3. _________ is a naturally occurring material that is broken down by processes of weathering and erosion, and is subsequently transported by the action of wind, water, or ice, and/or by the force of gravity acting on the particles. For example, silt falls out of suspension via sedimentation and forms soil (some of which may eventually become sedimentary rock).

   _________s are most often transported by water (fluvial processes), wind (aeolian processes) and glaciers.

   a. Mughal Empire
   b. Flood stage
   c. Streamflow
   d. Sediment

4. . _________ is a chemical compound with the chemical formula H_2CO_3 (equivalently OC_2). It is also a name sometimes given to solutions of carbon dioxide in water (carbonated water), because such solutions contain small amounts of H_2CO_3. In physiology, _________ is described as volatile acid or respiratory acid, because it is the only acid excreted as a gas by the lungs.

   a. Mughal Empire
   b. Carbonic acid
   c. Streamflow

5. Redox is a contraction of the name for a chemical reduction-_________ reaction. A reduction reaction always occurs with an _________ reaction. Redox reactions include all chemical reactions in which atoms have their _________ state changed; in general, redox reactions involve the transfer of electrons between chemical species.

   a. Essay on the Principle of Population
   b. Oxidation
   c. Streamflow
   d. African Union

ANSWER KEY
14. Weathering and Mass Wasting

1. b
2. a
3. d
4. b
5. b

---

15. Freshwater of the Continents

CHAPTER OUTLINE: KEY TERMS, PEOPLE, PLACES, CONCEPTS

Salinization

Evapotranspiration

Groundwater

Water table

Aquifer

Carbonic acid

Karst

Drainage system

Subsidence

Groundwater pollution

Saltwater intrusion

Pollution

Streamflow

Drainage basin

Stream

Stream gradient

Stream load

Turbulence

Channel

Rapid

River

15. Freshwater of the Continents

CHAPTER OUTLINE: KEY TERMS, PEOPLE, PLACES, CONCEPTS

- Flood stage
- Urban heat
- Urbanization
- Erosion
- Forest
- Lake
- National Forest
- Pond
- National Park
- Irrawaddy River
- Desalination
- Natural resource
- Eutrophication
- Thermal Pollution

15. Freshwater of the Continents

CHAPTER HIGHLIGHTS & NOTES: KEY TERMS, PEOPLE, PLACES, CONCEPTS

Salinization	Soil salinity is the salt content in the soil; the process of increasing the salt content is known as salinization. Salts occur naturally within soils and water. Salination can be caused by natural processes such as mineral weathering or by the gradual withdrawal of an ocean.
Evapotranspiration	Evapotranspiration is the sum of evaporation and plant transpiration from the Earth's land surface to atmosphere. Evaporation accounts for the movement of water to the air from sources such as the soil, canopy interception, and waterbodies. Transpiration accounts for the movement of water within a plant and the subsequent loss of water as vapor through stomata in its leaves.
Groundwater	Groundwater is the water present beneath Earth's surface in soil pore spaces and in the fractures of rock formations. A unit of rock or an unconsolidated deposit is called an aquifer when it can yield a usable quantity of water. The depth at which soil pore spaces or fractures and voids in rock become completely saturated with water is called the water table.
Water table	The water table is the surface where the water pressure head is equal to the atmospheric pressure . It may be conveniently visualized as the 'surface' of the subsurface materials that are saturated with groundwater in a given vicinity. However, saturated conditions may extend above the water table as surface tension holds water in some pores below atmospheric pressure.
Aquifer	An aquifer is an underground layer of water-bearing permeable rock or unconsolidated materials from which groundwater can be extracted using a water well. The study of water flow in aquifers and the characterization of aquifers is called hydrogeology. Related terms include aquitard, which is a bed of low permeability along an aquifer, and aquiclude (or aquifuge), which is a solid, impermeable area underlying or overlying an aquifer.
Carbonic acid	Carbonic acid is a chemical compound with the chemical formula H_2CO_3 (equivalently OC_2). It is also a name sometimes given to solutions of carbon dioxide in water (carbonated water), because such solutions contain small amounts of H_2CO_3. In physiology, carbonic acid is described as volatile acid or respiratory acid, because it is the only acid excreted as a gas by the lungs.
Karst	Karst topography is a landscape formed from the dissolution of soluble rocks such as limestone, dolomite, and gypsum. It is characterized by underground drainage systems with sinkholes and caves. It has also been documented for weathering-resistant rocks, such as quartzite, given the right conditions.
Drainage system	In geomorphology, a drainage system is the pattern formed by the streams, rivers, and lakes in a particular drainage basin. They are governed by the topography of the land, whether a particular region is dominated by hard or soft rocks, and the gradient of the land. Geomorphologists and hydrologists often view streams as being part of drainage basins.

15. Freshwater of the Continents

CHAPTER HIGHLIGHTS & NOTES: KEY TERMS, PEOPLE, PLACES, CONCEPTS

Subsidence	Subsidence in the Earth's atmosphere is most commonly caused by low temperatures: as air cools, it becomes denser and moves towards the ground, just as warm air becomes less dense and moves upwards. Cool subsiding air is subject to adiabatic warming which tends to cause the evaporation of any clouds that might be present. Subsidence generally causes high barometric pressure as more air moves into the same space: the polar highs are areas of almost constant subsidence, as are the horse latitudes, and these areas of subsidence are the sources of much of the world's prevailing wind.
Groundwater pollution	Groundwater pollution occurs when pollutants are released to the ground and make their way down into groundwater. It can also occur naturally due to the presence of a minor and unwanted constituent, contaminant or impurity in the groundwater, in which case it is more likely referred to as contamination rather than pollution. The pollutant creates a contaminant plume within an aquifer.
Saltwater intrusion	Saltwater intrusion is the movement of saline water into freshwater aquifers, which can lead to contamination of drinking water sources and other consequences. Saltwater intrusion occurs naturally to some degree in most coastal aquifers, owing to the hydraulic connection between groundwater and seawater. Because saltwater has a higher mineral content than freshwater, it is denser and has a higher water pressure.
Pollution	Pollution is the introduction of contaminants into the natural environment that cause adverse change. Pollution can take the form of chemical substances or energy, such as noise, heat or light. Pollutants, the components of pollution, can be either foreign substances/energies or naturally occurring contaminants.
Streamflow	Streamflow, or channel runoff, is the flow of water in streams, rivers, and other channels, and is a major element of the water cycle. It is one component of the runoff of water from the land to waterbodies, the other component being surface runoff. Water flowing in channels comes from surface runoff from adjacent hillslopes, from groundwater flow out of the ground, and from water discharged from pipes.
Drainage basin	A drainage basin or catchment basin is an extent or an area of land where all surface water from rain, melting snow, or ice converges to a single point at a lower elevation, usually the exit of the basin, where the waters join another body of water, such as a river, lake, reservoir, estuary, wetland, sea, or ocean. Thus if a tributary stream joins a brook that in turn joins a small river which is a tributary of a larger river, there is a series of successively larger (and lower elevation) drainage basins. For instance, the Missouri and Ohio rivers are within their own drainage basins and also within the drainage basin of the Mississippi River.
Stream	A stream is a body of water with a current, confined within a bed and stream banks.

Depending on its locale or certain characteristics, a stream may be referred to as a branch, brook, beck, burn, creek, 'crick', gill . In full flood the stream may or may not be 'torrential' in the dramatic sense of the word, but there will be one or more seasons in which the flow is reduced to a trickle or less.

Stream gradient

Stream gradient is the grade measured by the ratio of drop in elevation of a stream per unit horizontal distance, usually expressed as feet per mile or metres per kilometre.

Stream load

Stream load is a geologic term referring to the solid matter carried by a stream . Erosion and bed shear stress continually remove mineral material from the bed and banks of the stream channel, adding this material to the regular flow of water. The amount of solid load that a stream can carry, or stream capacity, is measured in metric tons per day, passing a given location.

Turbulence

In fluid dynamics, turbulence or turbulent flow is a flow regime characterized by chaotic property changes. This includes low momentum diffusion, high momentum convection, and rapid variation of pressure and flow velocity in space and time.

Flow in which the kinetic energy dies out due to the action of fluid molecular viscosity is called laminar flow.

Channel

In physical geography, a channel is a type of landform consisting of the outline of a path of relatively shallow and narrow body of fluid, most commonly the confine of a river, river delta or strait.

Channels can be either natural or human-made. A channel is typically outlined in terms of its bed and banks.

Rapid

A rapid is a section of a river where the river bed has a relatively steep gradient, causing an increase in water velocity and turbulence. A rapid is a hydrological feature between a run (a smoothly flowing part of a stream) and a cascade. A rapid is characterised by the river becoming shallower and having some rocks exposed above the flow surface.

River

A river is a natural watercourse, usually freshwater, flowing towards an ocean, a lake, a sea, or another river. In a few cases, a river simply flows into the ground or dries up completely at the end of its course, and does not reach another body of water. Small rivers may be called by several other names, including stream, creek, brook, rivulet, and rill.

Flood stage

Flood stage is the level at which a body of water's surface has risen to a sufficient level to cause sufficient inundation of areas that are not normally covered by water, causing an inconvenience or a threat to life and/or property. When a body of water rises to this level, it is considered a flood event. Flood stage does not apply to areal flooding.

15. Freshwater of the Continents

CHAPTER HIGHLIGHTS & NOTES: KEY TERMS, PEOPLE, PLACES, CONCEPTS

Urban heat	An urban heat island is a city or metropolitan area that is significantly warmer than its surrounding rural areas due to human activities. The phenomenon was first investigated and described by Luke Howard in the 1810s, although he was not the one to name the phenomenon. The temperature difference usually is larger at night than during the day, and is most apparent when winds are weak.
Urbanization	Urbanization is a population shift from rural to urban areas, 'the gradual increase in the proportion of people living in urban areas', and the ways in which each society adapts to the change. It predominantly results in the physical growth of urban areas, be it horizontal or vertical. The United Nations projected that half of the world's population would live in urban areas at the end of 2008. It is predicted that by 2050 about 64% of the developing world and 86% of the developed world will be urbanized.That is equivalent to approximately 3 billion urbanites by 2050, much of which will occur in Africa and Asia.
Erosion	In earth science, erosion is the action of surface processes that remove soil, rock, or dissolved material from one location on the Earth's crust, then transport it away to another location. The particulate breakdown of rock or soil into clastic sediment is referred to as physical or mechanical erosion; this contrasts with chemical erosion, where soil or rock material is removed from an area by its dissolving into a solvent (typically water), followed by the flow away of that solution. Eroded sediment or solutes may be transported just a few millimetres, or for thousands of kilometres.
Forest	A forest, also referred to as a wood or the woods, is an area with a high density of trees. As with cities, depending on various cultural definitions, what is considered a forest may vary significantly in size and have different classifications according to how and of what the forest is composed. A forest is usually an area filled with trees but any tall densely packed area of vegetation may be considered a forest, even underwater vegetation such as kelp forests, or non-vegetation such as fungi, and bacteria.
Lake	A lake is a body of relatively still water of considerable size, localized in a basin, that is surrounded by land apart from a river, stream, or other form of moving water that serves to feed or drain the lake. Lakes are inland and not part of the ocean and therefore are distinct from lagoons, and are larger and deeper than ponds. Lakes can be contrasted with rivers or streams, which are usually flowing.
National Forest	The National Forest is an environmental project in central England run by the National Forest Company. Portions of Leicestershire, Derbyshire and Staffordshire, 200 square miles (520 km^2) are being planted, in an attempt to blend ancient woodland with new plantings to create a new national forest. It stretches from the outskirts of Leicester in the east to Burton upon Trent in the west, and is planned link the ancient forests of Needwood and Charnwood.
Pond	A pond is a body of standing water, either natural or man-made, that is usually smaller than a lake.

They may arise naturally in floodplains as part of a river system, or they may be somewhat isolated depressions (examples include vernal pools and prairie potholes). Usually they contain shallow water with marsh and aquatic plants and animals.

National Park

A national park is a park in use for conservation purposes. Often it is a reserve of natural, semi-natural, or developed land that a sovereign state declares or owns. Although individual nations designate their own national parks differently, there is a common idea: the conservation of 'wild nature' for posterity and as a symbol of national pride.

Irrawaddy River

The Irrawaddy River or Ayeyarwady River is a river that flows from north to south through Burma (Myanmar). It is the country's largest river and most important commercial waterway. Originating from the confluence of the N'mai and Mali rivers, it flows relatively straight North-South before emptying through the Irrawaddy Delta into the Andaman Sea.

Desalination

Desalination or desalinization is a process that removes minerals from saline water. More generally, desalination may also refer to the removal of salts and minerals, as in soil desalination, which also happens to be a major issue for agricultural production.

Salt water is desalinated to produce fresh water suitable for human consumption or irrigation.

Natural resource

Natural Resources are all that exists without the actions of humankind. This includes all natural characteristics such as magnetic, gravitational, and electrical properties and forces. On earth we include sunlight, atmosphere, water, land (includes all minerals) along with all vegetation and animal life that naturally subsists upon or within the heretofore identified characteristics and substances.

Eutrophication

Eutrophication or more precisely hypertrophication, is the ecosystem response to the addition of artificial or natural substances, such as nitrates and phosphates, through fertilizers or sewage, to an aquatic system. One example is the 'bloom' or great increase of phytoplankton in a water body as a response to increased levels of nutrients. Negative environmental effects include hypoxia, the depletion of oxygen in the water, which induces reductions in specific fish and other animal populations.

Thermal Pollution

Thermal pollution is the degradation of water quality by any process that changes ambient water temperature. A common cause of thermal pollution is the use of water as a coolant by power plants and industrial manufacturers. When water used as a coolant is returned to the natural environment at a higher temperature, the change in temperature decreases oxygen supply and affects ecosystem composition.

15. Freshwater of the Continents

CHAPTER QUIZ: KEY TERMS, PEOPLE, PLACES, CONCEPTS

1. _________ is the introduction of contaminants into the natural environment that cause adverse change. _________ can take the form of chemical substances or energy, such as noise, heat or light. Pollutants, the components of _________, can be either foreign substances/energies or naturally occurring contaminants.

   a. Mughal Empire
   b. Biometeorology
   c. Clear-air turbulence
   d. Pollution

2. An _________ island is a city or metropolitan area that is significantly warmer than its surrounding rural areas due to human activities. The phenomenon was first investigated and described by Luke Howard in the 1810s, although he was not the one to name the phenomenon. The temperature difference usually is larger at night than during the day, and is most apparent when winds are weak.

   a. Essay on the Principle of Population
   b. African Union
   c. Urban heat
   d. Brine pool

3. The _________ is the surface where the water pressure head is equal to the atmospheric pressure . It may be conveniently visualized as the 'surface' of the subsurface materials that are saturated with groundwater in a given vicinity. However, saturated conditions may extend above the _________ as surface tension holds water in some pores below atmospheric pressure.

   a. salinization
   b. Water table
   c. Mughal Empire
   d. Climate classification

4. In earth science, _________ is the action of surface processes that remove soil, rock, or dissolved material from one location on the Earth's crust, then transport it away to another location. The particulate breakdown of rock or soil into clastic sediment is referred to as physical or mechanical _________; this contrasts with chemical _________, where soil or rock material is removed from an area by its dissolving into a solvent (typically water), followed by the flow away of that solution. Eroded sediment or solutes may be transported just a few millimetres, or for thousands of kilometres.

   a. Essay on the Principle of Population
   b. Erosion
   c. Islam
   d. Brine pool

5. . An _________ is an underground layer of water-bearing permeable rock or unconsolidated materials from which groundwater can be extracted using a water well. The study of water flow in _________s and the characterization of _________s is called hydrogeology.

Related terms include aquitard, which is a bed of low permeability along an _________, and aquiclude (or aquifuge), which is a solid, impermeable area underlying or overlying an _________.

a. Body of water
b. Aquifer
c. Guinean Forests of West Africa
d. Guinean forest-savanna mosaic

ANSWER KEY
15. Freshwater of the Continents

---

1. d
2. c
3. b
4. b
5. b

---

16. Landforms Made by Running Water

CHAPTER OUTLINE: KEY TERMS, PEOPLE, PLACES, CONCEPTS

- Soil erosion
- Erosion
- Water slope
- Peninsula
- River
- Colluvium
- Stream
- Alluvium
- Bed load
- Corrosion
- Dissolved load
- Stream load
- Transpiration stream
- Meander
- Downcutting
- Remote sensing
- Base level
- Peneplain
- Fluvial
- Aggradation
- SPRING

16. Landforms Made by Running Water

CHAPTER OUTLINE: KEY TERMS, PEOPLE, PLACES, CONCEPTS

______ Arid

______ Irrawaddy River

______ Climate

______ Desert

______ Sonoran Desert

CHAPTER HIGHLIGHTS & NOTES: KEY TERMS, PEOPLE, PLACES, CONCEPTS

Soil erosion	Soil erosion is one form of soil degradation. Soil erosion is a naturally occurring process on all land. The agents of soil erosion are water and wind, each contributing a significant amount of soil loss each year.
Erosion	In earth science, erosion is the action of surface processes that remove soil, rock, or dissolved material from one location on the Earth's crust, then transport it away to another location. The particulate breakdown of rock or soil into clastic sediment is referred to as physical or mechanical erosion; this contrasts with chemical erosion, where soil or rock material is removed from an area by its dissolving into a solvent (typically water), followed by the flow away of that solution. Eroded sediment or solutes may be transported just a few millimetres, or for thousands of kilometres.
Water slope	A water slope is a type of canal inclined plane built to carry boats from a canal or river at one elevation up to or down to a canal or river at another elevation.
Peninsula	A peninsula is a piece of land that is bordered by water on three sides but connected to mainland. The surrounding water is usually understood to belong to a single, contiguous body, but is not always explicitly defined as such. In many Germanic and Celtic languages and also in Baltic, Slavic, Hungarian, Chinese, Hebrew and Korean, peninsulas are called 'half-islands'.
River	A river is a natural watercourse, usually freshwater, flowing towards an ocean, a lake, a sea, or another river. In a few cases, a river simply flows into the ground or dries up completely at the end of its course, and does not reach another body of water. Small rivers may be called by several other names, including stream, creek, brook, rivulet, and rill.

Term	Description
Colluvium	Colluvium is a general name for loose, unconsolidated sediments that have been deposited at the base of hillslopes by either rainwash, sheetwash, slow continuous downslope creep, or a variable combination of these processes. Colluvium is typically composed of a heterogeneous range of rock types and sediments ranging from silt to rock fragments of various sizes. This term is also used to specifically refer to sediment deposited at the base of a hillslope by unconcentrated surface runoff or sheet erosion.
Stream	A stream is a body of water with a current, confined within a bed and stream banks. Depending on its locale or certain characteristics, a stream may be referred to as a branch, brook, beck, burn, creek, 'crick', gill . In full flood the stream may or may not be 'torrential' in the dramatic sense of the word, but there will be one or more seasons in which the flow is reduced to a trickle or less.
Alluvium	Alluvium is loose, unconsolidated (not cemented together into a solid rock) soil or sediments, which has been eroded, reshaped by water in some form, and redeposited in a non-marine setting. Alluvium is typically made up of a variety of materials, including fine particles of silt and clay and larger particles of sand and gravel. When this loose alluvial material is deposited or cemented into a lithological unit, or lithified, it is called an alluvial deposit.
Bed load	The term bed load or bedload describes particles in a flowing fluid that are transported along the bed. Bed load is complementary to suspended load and wash load. Bed load moves by rolling, sliding, and/or saltating (hopping).
Corrosion	Corrosion is a natural process, which converts a refined metal to a more stable form, such as its oxide, hydroxide, or sulfide. It is the gradual destruction of materials (usually metals) by chemical reaction with their environment. Corrosion engineering is the field dedicated to controlling and stopping corrosion.
Dissolved load	Dissolved load is material, especially ions from chemical weathering, that are carried in solution by a stream. The dissolved load contributes to the total amount of material removed from a catchment. The amount of material carried as dissolved load is typically much smaller than the suspended load, though this is not always the case particularly when the available river flow is mostly harnessed for irrigation, industrial, etc.
Stream load	Stream load is a geologic term referring to the solid matter carried by a stream . Erosion and bed shear stress continually remove mineral material from the bed and banks of the stream channel, adding this material to the regular flow of water. The amount of solid load that a stream can carry, or stream capacity, is measured in metric tons per day, passing a given location.
Transpiration stream	In plants, the transpiration stream is the uninterrupted stream of water and solutes which is taken up by the roots and transported via the xylem vessels to the leaves where it evaporates into the air/apoplast-interface of the substomatal cavity.

16. Landforms Made by Running Water

It is driven by capillary action and in some plants by root pressure. The main driving factor is the difference in water potential between the soil and the substomatal cavity caused by transpiration.

Meander	A meander, in general, is a bend in a sinuous watercourse or river. A meander is formed when the moving water in a stream erodes the outer banks and widens its valley and the inner part of the river has less energy and deposits what it is carrying. A stream of any volume may assume a meandering course, alternately eroding sediments from the outside of a bend and depositing them on the inside.
Downcutting	Downcutting, also called erosional downcutting, downward erosion or vertical erosion is a geological process that deepens the channel of a stream or valley by removing material from the stream's bed or the valley's floor. The speed of downcutting depends on the stream's base level, the lowest point to which the stream can erode. Sea level is the ultimate base level, but many streams have a higher 'temporary' base level because they empty into another body of water that is above sea level or encounter bedrock that resists erosion.
Remote sensing	Remote sensing is the acquisition of information about an object or phenomenon without making physical contact with the object. In modern usage, the term generally refers to the use of aerial sensor technologies to detect and classify objects on Earth (both on the surface, and in the atmosphere and oceans) by means of propagated signals (e.g. electromagnetic radiation). It may be split into active remote sensing, when a signal is first emitted from aircraft or satellites) or passive (e.g. sunlight) when information is merely recorded.
Base level	The base level of a river or stream is the lowest point to which it can flow, often referred to as the 'mouth of the river'. For large rivers, sea level is usually the base level, but a large river or lake is likewise the base level for tributary streams. All rivers and streams erode toward sea level, which is also known as the 'ultimate base level.' A rather rare exception can be seen in the Jordan River, for which the base level is the Dead Sea, 417 m below modern sea level.
Peneplain	In geomorphology and geology a peneplain is a low-relief non-constructional plain. This is the definition in the broadest of terms, albeit with frequency the usage of peneplain is meant to imply the representation of a near-final (or penultimate) stage of fluvial erosion during times of extended tectonic stability. Peneplains are sometimes associated with the cycle of erosion theory of William Morris Davis.
Fluvial	Fluvial is a term used in geography and geology to refer to the processes associated with rivers and streams and the deposits and landforms created by them. When the stream or rivers are associated with glaciers, ice sheets, or ice caps, the term glaciofluvial or fluvioglacial is used.
Aggradation	Aggradation is the term used in geology for the increase in land elevation, typically in a river system, due to the deposition of sediment. Aggradation occurs in areas in which the supply of sediment is greater than the amount of material that the system is able to transport.

SPRING	SPRING is a freeware GIS and remote sensing image processing system with an object-oriented data model which provides for the integration of raster and vector data representations in a single environment. It has Windows and Linux versions and provides a comprehensive set of functions, including tools for Satellite Image Processing, Digital Terrain Modeling, Spatial Analysis, Geostatistics, Spatial Statistics, Spatial Databases and Map Management. SPRING is a product of Brazilian National Institute for Space Research (INPE), who is developing SPRING since 1992, and has required over 200 man/years of development and includes extensive documentation, tutorials and examples.
Arid	A region is arid when it is characterized by a severe lack of available water, to the extent of hindering or preventing the growth and development of plant and animal life. Environments subject to arid climates tend to lack vegetation and are called xeric or desertic. Most 'arid' climates surround the equator; these places include most of Africa and parts of South America, Central America and Australia.
Irrawaddy River	The Irrawaddy River or Ayeyarwady River is a river that flows from north to south through Burma (Myanmar). It is the country's largest river and most important commercial waterway. Originating from the confluence of the N'mai and Mali rivers, it flows relatively straight North-South before emptying through the Irrawaddy Delta into the Andaman Sea.
Climate	Climate is a measure of the average pattern of variation in temperature, humidity, atmospheric pressure, wind, precipitation, atmospheric particle count and other meteorological variables in a given region over long periods of time. Climate is different than weather, in that weather only describes the short-term conditions of these variables in a given region. A region's climate is generated by the climate system, which has five components: atmosphere, hydrosphere, cryosphere, land surface, and biosphere.
Desert	A desert is a barren area of land where little precipitation occurs and consequently living conditions are hostile for plant and animal life. The lack of vegetation exposes the unprotected surface of the ground to the processes of denudation. About one third of the land surface of the world is arid or semi-arid.
Sonoran Desert	The Sonoran Desert is a North American desert which covers large parts of the Southwestern United States in Arizona and California, and of Northwestern Mexico in Sonora, Baja California and Baja California Sur. It is one of the largest and hottest deserts in North America, with an area of 311,000 square kilometers (120,000 sq mi). The western portion of the United States-Mexico border passes through the Sonoran Desert.

16. Landforms Made by Running Water

CHAPTER QUIZ: KEY TERMS, PEOPLE, PLACES, CONCEPTS

1. _________, also called erosional _________, downward erosion or vertical erosion is a geological process that deepens the channel of a stream or valley by removing material from the stream's bed or the valley's floor. The speed of _________ depends on the stream's base level, the lowest point to which the stream can erode. Sea level is the ultimate base level, but many streams have a higher 'temporary' base level because they empty into another body of water that is above sea level or encounter bedrock that resists erosion.

   a. Downcutting
   b. Stream load
   c. Mughal Empire
   d. Braid bar

2. A _________ is a type of canal inclined plane built to carry boats from a canal or river at one elevation up to or down to a canal or river at another elevation.

   a. Water slope
   b. Russian Empire
   c. Survival International
   d. Basilica of Our Lady of Peace

3. _________ is one form of soil degradation. _________ is a naturally occurring process on all land. The agents of _________ are water and wind, each contributing a significant amount of soil loss each year.

   a. Mughal Empire
   b. Russian Empire
   c. Survival International
   d. Soil erosion

4. In geomorphology and geology a _________ is a low-relief non-constructional plain. This is the definition in the broadest of terms, albeit with frequency the usage of _________ is meant to imply the representation of a near-final (or penultimate) stage of fluvial erosion during times of extended tectonic stability. _________s are sometimes associated with the cycle of erosion theory of William Morris Davis.

   a. Peneplain
   b. Hydraulic action
   c. Stream load
   d. Russian Empire

5. . _________ is material, especially ions from chemical weathering, that are carried in solution by a stream. The _________ contributes to the total amount of material removed from a catchment. The amount of material carried as _________ is typically much smaller than the suspended load, though this is not always the case particularly when the available river flow is mostly harnessed for irrigation, industrial, etc.

   a. Mughal Empire
   b. Gelifluction

c. Suspended load

d. Dissolved load

ANSWER KEY
16. Landforms Made by Running Water

1. a
2. a
3. d
4. a
5. d

---

17. Landforms Made by Waves and Wind

CHAPTER OUTLINE: KEY TERMS, PEOPLE, PLACES, CONCEPTS

- Desert
- Climate change
- Biogeography
- Coastal erosion
- Geography
- Global change
- Coral
- Coral reef
- Subsidence
- Land
- Sea level
- Arctic
- Wind
- Fetch
- Suspended load
- Littoral drift
- Longshore drift
- Littoral
- Tide
- Wind wave
- Tidal range

17. Landforms Made by Waves and Wind

CHAPTER OUTLINE: KEY TERMS, PEOPLE, PLACES, CONCEPTS

- Tsunami
- Coastline
- Island
- Sea cave
- National Park
- Marine terrace
- Dune
- Foredune
- Progradation
- Barrier island
- Baymouth bar
- Spit
- Tombolo
- Bank
- Lagoon
- Fiord
- Fiordland
- Atoll
- Coastal engineering
- Fringing reef
- Deep ocean

17. Landforms Made by Waves and Wind

CHAPTER OUTLINE: KEY TERMS, PEOPLE, PLACES, CONCEPTS

- Desert pavement
- Erosion
- Rip-rap
- Ocean current
- Transpiration
- SPRING

CHAPTER HIGHLIGHTS & NOTES: KEY TERMS, PEOPLE, PLACES, CONCEPTS

Desert	A desert is a barren area of land where little precipitation occurs and consequently living conditions are hostile for plant and animal life. The lack of vegetation exposes the unprotected surface of the ground to the processes of denudation. About one third of the land surface of the world is arid or semi-arid.
Climate change	Climate change is a significant and lasting change in the statistical distribution of weather patterns over periods ranging from decades to millions of years. It may be a change in average weather conditions, or in the distribution of weather around the average conditions (i.e., more or fewer extreme weather events). Climate change is caused by factors such as biotic processes, variations in solar radiation received by Earth, plate tectonics, and volcanic eruptions.
Biogeography	Biogeography is the study of the distribution of species and ecosystems in geographic space and through geological time. Organisms and biological communities vary in a highly regular fashion along geographic gradients of latitude, elevation, isolation and habitat area. Knowledge of spatial variation in the numbers and types of organisms is as vital to us today as it was to our early human ancestors, as we adapt to heterogeneous but geographically predictable environments.
Coastal erosion	Coastal erosion is the wearing away of land and the removal of beach or dune sediments by wave action, tidal currents, wave currents or drainage .

17. Landforms Made by Waves and Wind

CHAPTER HIGHLIGHTS & NOTES: KEY TERMS, PEOPLE, PLACES, CONCEPTS

Waves, generated by storms, wind, or fast moving motor craft, cause coastal erosion, which may take the form of long-term losses of sediment and rocks, or merely the temporary redistribution of coastal sediments; erosion in one location may result in accretion nearby. The study of erosion and sediment redistribution is called 'coastal morphodynamics'.

Geography

The Geography is Ptolemy's main work besides the Almagest. It is a treatise on cartography and a compilation of what was known about the world's geography in the Roman Empire of the 2nd century. Ptolemy relied mainly on the work of an earlier geographer, Marinos of Tyre, and on gazetteers of the Roman and ancient Persian empire.

Global change

Global change refers to planetary-scale changes in the Earth system. The system consists of the land, oceans, atmosphere, poles, life, the planet's natural cycles and deep Earth processes. These constituent parts influence one another.

Coral

Corals are marine invertebrates in class Anthozoa of phylum Cnidaria typically living in compact colonies of many identical individual 'polyps'. The group includes the important reef builders that inhabit tropical oceans and secrete calcium carbonate to form a hard skeleton.

A coral 'head' is a colony of myriad genetically identical polyps.

Coral reef

Coral reefs are underwater structures made from calcium carbonate secreted by corals. Coral reefs are colonies of tiny animals found in marine waters that contain few nutrients. Most coral reefs are built from stony corals, which in turn consist of polyps that cluster in groups.

Subsidence

Subsidence in the Earth's atmosphere is most commonly caused by low temperatures: as air cools, it becomes denser and moves towards the ground, just as warm air becomes less dense and moves upwards. Cool subsiding air is subject to adiabatic warming which tends to cause the evaporation of any clouds that might be present. Subsidence generally causes high barometric pressure as more air moves into the same space: the polar highs are areas of almost constant subsidence, as are the horse latitudes, and these areas of subsidence are the sources of much of the world's prevailing wind.

Land

Land, sometimes referred to as dry land, is the solid surface of the Earth, that is not covered by water. The division between land and ocean, sea, or other bodies of water, is one of the most fundamental separations on the planet. The vast majority of human activity has historically occurred, and continues to occur, on land.

Sea level

Mean sea level is a datum representing the average height of the ocean's surface (such as the halfway point between the mean high tide and the mean low tide); used as a standard in reckoning land elevation. MSL also plays an important role in marine navigation as a chart datum and aviation, where standard sea level pressure is used as the measurement datum of altitude at flight levels.

17. Landforms Made by Waves and Wind

CHAPTER HIGHLIGHTS & NOTES: KEY TERMS, PEOPLE, PLACES, CONCEPTS

Arctic	The Arctic is a polar region located at the northernmost part of the Earth. The Arctic consists of the Arctic Ocean and parts of Alaska (United States), Canada, Finland, Greenland (Denmark), Iceland, Norway, Russia, and Sweden. The Arctic region consists of a vast ocean with a seasonally varying ice cover, surrounded by treeless permafrost.
Wind	Wind is the flow of gases on a large scale. On the surface of the Earth, wind consists of the bulk movement of air. In outer space, solar wind is the movement of gases or charged particles from the sun through space, while planetary wind is the outgassing of light chemical elements from a planet's atmosphere into space.
Fetch	The fetch, also called the fetch length, is the length of water over which a given wind has blown. Fetch is used in geography and meteorology and its effects are usually associated with sea state and when it reaches shore it is the main factor that creates storm surge which leads to coastal erosion and flooding. It also plays a large part in longshore drift as well.
Suspended load	Suspended load is the portion of the sediment that is carried by a fluid flow which settle slowly enough such that it almost never touches the bed. It is maintained in suspension by the turbulence in the flowing water and consists of particles generally of the fine sand, silt and clay size.
Littoral drift	Longshore drift is a geographical process that consists of the transportation of sediments along a coast at an angle to the shoreline, which is dependent on prevailing wind direction, swash and backwash. This process occurs in the littoral zone, and in or close to the surf zone. The process is also known as littoral drift, longshore current or longshore transport.
Longshore drift	Longshore drift consists of the transportation of sediments along a coast at an angle to the shoreline, which is dependent on prevailing wind direction, swash and backwash. This process occurs in the littoral zone, and in or close to the surf zone. The process is also known as longshore transport or littoral drift.
Littoral	The littoral zone is the part of a sea, lake or river that is close to the shore. In coastal environments the littoral zone extends from the high water mark, which is rarely inundated, to shoreline areas that are permanently submerged. It always includes this intertidal zone and is often used to mean the same as the intertidal zone.
Tide	Tides are the rise and fall of sea levels caused by the combined effects of the gravitational forces exerted by the Moon and the Sun and the rotation of the Earth. Some shorelines experience two almost equal high tides and two low tides each day, called a semi-diurnal tide. Some locations experience only one high and one low tide each day, called a diurnal tide.

17. Landforms Made by Waves and Wind

CHAPTER HIGHLIGHTS & NOTES: KEY TERMS, PEOPLE, PLACES, CONCEPTS

Wind wave	In fluid dynamics, wind waves or, more precisely, wind-generated waves are surface waves that occur on the free surface of oceans, seas, lakes, rivers, and canals or even on small puddles and ponds. They usually result from the wind blowing over a vast enough stretch of fluid surface. Waves in the oceans can travel thousands of miles before reaching land.
Tidal range	The tidal range is the vertical difference between the high tide and the succeeding low tide. Tides are the rise and fall of sea levels caused by the combined effects of the gravitational forces exerted by the Moon and the Sun and the rotation of the Earth. The tidal range is not constant, but changes depending on where the sun and the moon are.
Tsunami	A tsunami also known as a seismic sea wave, is a series of waves in a water body caused by the displacement of a large volume of water, generally in an ocean or a large lake. Earthquakes, volcanic eruptions and other underwater explosions (including detonations of underwater nuclear devices), landslides, glacier calvings, meteorite impacts and other disturbances above or below water all have the potential to generate a tsunami.
Coastline	A coastline or a seashore is the area where land meets the sea or ocean, or a line that forms the boundary between the land and the ocean or a lake. A precise line that can be called a coastline cannot be determined due to the Coastline paradox. The term coastal zone is a region where interaction of the sea and land processes occurs.
Island	An island or isle is any piece of sub-continental land that is surrounded by water. Very small islands such as emergent land features on atolls can be called islets, skerries, cays or keys. An island in a river or a lake island may be called an eyot or ait, or a holm.
Sea cave	A sea cave, also known as a littoral cave, is a type of cave formed primarily by the wave action of the sea. The primary process involved is erosion. Sea caves are found throughout the world, actively forming along present coastlines and as relict sea caves on former coastlines.
National Park	A national park is a park in use for conservation purposes. Often it is a reserve of natural, semi-natural, or developed land that a sovereign state declares or owns. Although individual nations designate their own national parks differently, there is a common idea: the conservation of 'wild nature' for posterity and as a symbol of national pride.
Marine terrace	A marine terrace, coastal terrace, raised beach or perched coastline is a relatively flat, horizontal or gently inclined surface of marine origin, mostly an old abrasion platform which has been lifted out of the sphere of wave activity . Thus it lies above or under the current sea level, depending on its time of formation. It is bounded by a steeper ascending slope on the landward side and a steeper descending slope on the seaward side (sometimes called 'riser').
Dune	In physical geography, a dune is a hill of sand built either by wind or water flow. Dunes occur in different forms and sizes, formed by interaction with the flow of air or water.

17. Landforms Made by Waves and Wind

CHAPTER HIGHLIGHTS & NOTES: KEY TERMS, PEOPLE, PLACES, CONCEPTS

Foredune	A foredune is a kind of dune ridge that runs parallel to the shore of an ocean, lake, bay, or estuary. Foredunes consist of sand deposited by wind on a vegetated part of the shore. Foredunes can be classified generally as incipient or established.
Progradation	In sedimentary geology and geomorphology, the term progradation refers to the growth of a river delta farther out into the sea over time. This occurs when the mass balance of sediment into the delta is such that the volume of incoming sediment is greater than the volume of the delta that is lost through subsidence, sea-level rise, and/or erosion.
Barrier island	Barrier Islands, a coastal landform and a type of barrier system, are exceptionally flat and lumpy areas of sand, that are parallel to the mainland coast. They usually occur in chains, consisting of anything from a few islands to more than a dozen. Excepting the tidal inlets that separate the islands, a barrier chain may extend uninterrupted for over a hundred kilometers, the longest and widest being Padre Island.
Baymouth bar	A baymouth bar is a depositional feature as a result of longshore drift. It is a spit that completely closes access to a bay, thus sealing it off from the main body of water. These bars usually consist of accumulated gravel and sand carried by the current of longshore drift and deposited at a less turbulent part of the current.
Spit	A spit or sandspit is a deposition landform found off coasts. At one end, spits connect to a head, and extend into the nose. A spit is a type of bar or beach that develops where a re-entrant occurs, such as at cove's headlands, by the process of longshore drift.
Tombolo	A tombolo, from the Italian tombolo, derived from the Latin tumulus, meaning 'mound,' and sometimes translated as ayre, is a deposition landform in which an island is attached to the mainland by a narrow piece of land such as a spit or bar. Once attached, the island is then known as a tied island. Several islands tied together by bars which rise above the water level are called a tombolo cluster.
Bank	In geography a bank generally refers to the land alongside a body of water. Various structures are referred to as banks in different fields of geography. In limnology, the study of inland waters, a stream bank or river bank is the terrain alongside the bed of a river, creek, or stream.
Lagoon	A lagoon is a shallow body of water separated from a larger body of water by barrier islands or reefs. Lagoons are commonly divided into coastal lagoons and atoll lagoons. They have also been identified as occurring on mixed-sand and gravel coastlines.
Fiord	Geologically, a fjord or fiord is a long, narrow inlet with steep sides or cliffs, created by glacial erosion.

There are many fjords on the coasts of Alaska, British Columbia, Chile, Greenland, Iceland, the Kerguelen Islands, New Zealand, Norway, Labrador, Nunavut, Newfoundland, and Washington state. Norway's coastline is estimated at 29,000 km with fjords, but only 2500 km when fjords are excluded.

Fiordland

Fiordland is a geographic region of New Zealand that is situated on the south-western corner of the South Island, comprising the western-most third of Southland. Most of Fiordland is dominated by the steep sides of the snow-capped Southern Alps, deep lakes and its ocean-flooded, steep western valleys. Indeed, the name 'Fiordland' comes from a variant spelling of the Scandinavian word for this type of steep valley, 'fjord'.

Atoll

An atoll is a ring-shaped coral reef including a coral rim that encircles a lagoon partially or completely. There may be coral islands/cays on the coral rim.

Coastal engineering

Coastal engineering is the branch of civil engineering concerning the specific demands posed by constructing at or near the coast, as well as the development of the coast itself.

The hydrodynamic impact of especially waves, tides, storm surges and tsunamis and the harsh environment of salt seawater are typical challenges for the coastal engineer - as are the morphodynamic changes of the coastal topography, caused both by the autonomous development of the system and man-made changes. The areas of interest in coastal engineering include the coasts of the oceans, seas, marginal seas, estuaries and big lakes.

Fringing reef

A fringing reef is one of the three main types of coral reefs recognized by most coral reef scientists. It is distinguished from the other two main types (barrier reefs and atolls) in that it has either an entirely shallow backreef zone (lagoon) or none at all. If a fringing reef grows directly from the shoreline the reef flat extends right to the beach and there is no backreef.

Deep ocean

The deep sea or deep layer is the lowest layer in the ocean, existing below the thermocline and above the seabed, at a depth of 1000 fathoms or more. Little or no light penetrates this part of the ocean, and most of the organisms that live there rely for subsistence on falling organic matter produced in the photic zone. For this reason, scientists once assumed that life would be sparse in the deep ocean, but virtually every probe has revealed that, on the contrary, life is abundant in the deep ocean.

Desert pavement

A desert pavement, also called reg, serir (eastern Sahara), gibber (in Australia), or saï (central Asia) is a desert surface covered with closely packed, interlocking angular or rounded rock fragments of pebble and cobble size. They typically top alluvial fans. Desert varnish collects on the exposed surface rocks over time.

Erosion

In earth science, erosion is the action of surface processes that remove soil, rock, or dissolved material from one location on the Earth's crust, then transport it away to another location.

The particulate breakdown of rock or soil into clastic sediment is referred to as physical or mechanical erosion; this contrasts with chemical erosion, where soil or rock material is removed from an area by its dissolving into a solvent (typically water), followed by the flow away of that solution. Eroded sediment or solutes may be transported just a few millimetres, or for thousands of kilometres.

Rip-rap

Riprap, also known as rip rap, rip-rap, shot rock, rock armour or rubble, is rock or other material used to armor shorelines, streambeds, bridge abutments, pilings and other shoreline structures against scour and water or ice erosion. It is made from a variety of rock types, commonly granite or limestone, and occasionally concrete rubble from building and paving demolition. It can be used on any waterway or water containment where there is potential for water erosion.

Ocean current

An ocean current is a continuous, directed movement of seawater generated by the forces acting upon this mean flow, such as breaking waves, wind, Coriolis effect, cabbeling, temperature and salinity differences and tides caused by the gravitational pull of the Moon and the Sun. Depth contours, shoreline configurations and interaction with other currents influence a current's direction and strength. A deep current is any ocean current at a depth of greater than 100m.

Transpiration

Transpiration is the process of water movement through a plant and its evaporation from aerial parts, such as leaves, stems and flowers. Water is necessary for plants but only a small amount of water taken up by the roots is used for growth and metabolism. The remaining 97-99.5% is lost by transpiration and guttation.

SPRING

SPRING is a freeware GIS and remote sensing image processing system with an object-oriented data model which provides for the integration of raster and vector data representations in a single environment. It has Windows and Linux versions and provides a comprehensive set of functions, including tools for Satellite Image Processing, Digital Terrain Modeling, Spatial Analysis, Geostatistics, Spatial Statistics, Spatial Databases and Map Management.

SPRING is a product of Brazilian National Institute for Space Research (INPE), who is developing SPRING since 1992, and has required over 200 man/years of development and includes extensive documentation, tutorials and examples.

17. Landforms Made by Waves and Wind

CHAPTER QUIZ: KEY TERMS, PEOPLE, PLACES, CONCEPTS

1. _________ is the branch of civil engineering concerning the specific demands posed by constructing at or near the coast, as well as the development of the coast itself.

   The hydrodynamic impact of especially waves, tides, storm surges and tsunamis and the harsh environment of salt seawater are typical challenges for the coastal engineer - as are the morphodynamic changes of the coastal topography, caused both by the autonomous development of the system and man-made changes. The areas of interest in _________ include the coasts of the oceans, seas, marginal seas, estuaries and big lakes.

   a. Coastal engineering
   b. Porcupine Abyssal Plain
   c. Sigsbee Deep
   d. Sohm Abyssal Plain

2. An _________ is a ring-shaped coral reef including a coral rim that encircles a lagoon partially or completely. There may be coral islands/cays on the coral rim.

   a. Naturaliste Plateau
   b. Porcupine Abyssal Plain
   c. Atoll
   d. Sohm Abyssal Plain

3. _________ is a geographic region of New Zealand that is situated on the south-western corner of the South Island, comprising the western-most third of Southland. Most of _________ is dominated by the steep sides of the snow-capped Southern Alps, deep lakes and its ocean-flooded, steep western valleys. Indeed, the name '_________' comes from a variant spelling of the Scandinavian word for this type of steep valley, 'fjord'.

   a. Teniente Luis Carvajal Villaroel Antarctic Base
   b. Guinean Forests of West Africa
   c. Guinean forest-savanna mosaic
   d. Fiordland

4. A _________, from the Italian _________, derived from the Latin tumulus, meaning 'mound,' and sometimes translated as ayre, is a deposition landform in which an island is attached to the mainland by a narrow piece of land such as a spit or bar. Once attached, the island is then known as a tied island. Several islands tied together by bars which rise above the water level are called a _________ cluster.

   a. Tombolo
   b. Naturaliste Plateau
   c. Porcupine Abyssal Plain
   d. Sigsbee Deep

5. . An _________ or isle is any piece of sub-continental land that is surrounded by water. Very small _________s such as emergent land features on atolls can be called islets, skerries, cays or keys.

An ________ in a river or a lake ________ may be called an eyot or ait, or a holm.

a. Naturaliste Plateau
b. Island
c. Sigsbee Deep
d. Sohm Abyssal Plain

ANSWER KEY

17. Landforms Made by Waves and Wind

---

1. a

2. c

3. d

4. a

5. b

---

18. Glacial and Periglacial Landforms

CHAPTER OUTLINE: KEY TERMS, PEOPLE, PLACES, CONCEPTS

- Antarctica
- Glacier
- Ice Sheet
- Global warming
- Sea ice
- Cirque
- Ice field
- National Park
- Firn
- Mass balance
- Basal sliding
- Climate change
- Climate
- Erosion
- Fiord
- Moraine
- Tarim Basin
- Remote sensing
- Lake
- Esker
- Till plain

18. Glacial and Periglacial Landforms

CHAPTER OUTLINE: KEY TERMS, PEOPLE, PLACES, CONCEPTS

- Alpine permafrost
- Permafrost
- Pluvial
- Active layer
- Island
- Gelifluction
- Patterned ground
- Thermokarst
- Periglacial
- SPRING
- Deep ocean
- Ice age
- Ocean current
- Weathering
- Current
- Trough
- Insolation
- Siberia

18. Glacial and Periglacial Landforms

CHAPTER HIGHLIGHTS & NOTES: KEY TERMS, PEOPLE, PLACES, CONCEPTS

Antarctica	Antarctica is Earth's southernmost continent, containing the geographic South Pole. It is situated in the Antarctic region of the Southern Hemisphere, almost entirely south of the Antarctic Circle, and is surrounded by the Southern Ocean. At 14.0 million km^2 (5.4 million sq mi), it is the fifth-largest continent in area after Asia, Africa, North America, and South America. For comparison, Antarctica is nearly twice the size of Australia.
Glacier	A glacier is a persistent body of dense ice that is constantly moving under its own weight; it forms where the accumulation of snow exceeds its ablation (melting and sublimation) over many years, often centuries. Glaciers slowly deform and flow due to stresses induced by their weight, creating crevasses, seracs, and other distinguishing features. They also abrade rock and debris from their substrate to create landforms such as cirques and moraines.
Ice Sheet	An ice sheet is a mass of glacier ice that covers surrounding terrain and is greater than 50,000 km^2, thus also known as continental glacier. The only current ice sheets are in Antarctica and Greenland; during the last glacial period at Last Glacial Maximum (LGM) the Laurentide ice sheet covered much of North America, the Weichselian ice sheet covered northern Europe and the Patagonian Ice Sheet covered southern South America. Ice sheets are bigger than ice shelves or alpine glaciers. Masses of ice covering less than 50,000 km^2 are termed an ice cap.
Global warming	Global warming is the rise in the average temperature of Earth's atmosphere and oceans since the late 19th century and its projected continuation. Since the early 20th century, Earth's mean surface temperature has increased by about 0.8 °C (1.4 °F), with about two-thirds of the increase occurring since 1980. Warming of the climate system is unequivocal, and scientists are 95-100% certain that it is primarily caused by increasing concentrations of greenhouse gases produced by human activities such as the burning of fossil fuels and deforestation. These findings are recognized by the national science academies of all major industrialized nations.
Sea ice	Sea ice arises as seawater freezes. Because ice is less dense than water, it floats on the ocean's surface (as does fresh water ice, which has an even lower density). Sea ice covers about 7% of the Earth's surface and about 12% of the world's oceans.
Cirque	A cirque is a theatre-like valley formed by glacial erosion. Alternative names for this landform are corrie (from Scottish Gaelic coire meaning a pot or cauldron) and cwm (Welsh for 'valley', pronounced coom). A cirque may also be a similarly shaped landform arising from fluvial erosion.
Ice field	An ice field is an area less than 50,000 km^2 (19,000 sq mi) of ice often found in the colder climates and higher altitudes of the world where there is sufficient precipitation. It is an extensive area of interconnected valley glaciers from which the higher peaks rise as nunataks.

18. Glacial and Periglacial Landforms

CHAPTER HIGHLIGHTS & NOTES: KEY TERMS, PEOPLE, PLACES, CONCEPTS

National Park	A national park is a park in use for conservation purposes. Often it is a reserve of natural, semi-natural, or developed land that a sovereign state declares or owns. Although individual nations designate their own national parks differently, there is a common idea: the conservation of 'wild nature' for posterity and as a symbol of national pride.
Firn	Firn is partially compacted névé, a type of snow that has been left over from past seasons and has been recrystallized into a substance denser than névé. It is ice that is at an intermediate stage between snow and glacial ice. Firn has the appearance of wet sugar, but has a hardness that makes it extremely resistant to shovelling.
Mass balance	A mass balance, also called a material balance, is an application of conservation of mass to the analysis of physical systems. By accounting for material entering and leaving a system, mass flows can be identified which might have been unknown, or difficult to measure without this technique. The exact conservation law used in the analysis of the system depends on the context of the problem, but all revolve around mass conservation, i.e. that matter cannot disappear or be created spontaneously.
Basal sliding	Basal sliding is the act of a glacier sliding over the bed due to meltwater under the ice acting as a lubricant. This movement very much depends on the temperature of the area, the slope of the glacier, the bed roughness, the amount of meltwater from the glacier, and the glacier's size. The movement that happens to these glaciers as they slide is that of a jerky motion where any seismic events, especially at the base of glacier, can cause movement.
Climate change	Climate change is a significant and lasting change in the statistical distribution of weather patterns over periods ranging from decades to millions of years. It may be a change in average weather conditions, or in the distribution of weather around the average conditions (i.e., more or fewer extreme weather events). Climate change is caused by factors such as biotic processes, variations in solar radiation received by Earth, plate tectonics, and volcanic eruptions.
Climate	Climate is a measure of the average pattern of variation in temperature, humidity, atmospheric pressure, wind, precipitation, atmospheric particle count and other meteorological variables in a given region over long periods of time. Climate is different than weather, in that weather only describes the short-term conditions of these variables in a given region. A region's climate is generated by the climate system, which has five components: atmosphere, hydrosphere, cryosphere, land surface, and biosphere.
Erosion	In earth science, erosion is the action of surface processes that remove soil, rock, or dissolved material from one location on the Earth's crust, then transport it away to another location.

	The particulate breakdown of rock or soil into clastic sediment is referred to as physical or mechanical erosion; this contrasts with chemical erosion, where soil or rock material is removed from an area by its dissolving into a solvent (typically water), followed by the flow away of that solution. Eroded sediment or solutes may be transported just a few millimetres, or for thousands of kilometres.
Fiord	Geologically, a fjord or fiord is a long, narrow inlet with steep sides or cliffs, created by glacial erosion. There are many fjords on the coasts of Alaska, British Columbia, Chile, Greenland, Iceland, the Kerguelen Islands, New Zealand, Norway, Labrador, Nunavut, Newfoundland, and Washington state. Norway's coastline is estimated at 29,000 km with fjords, but only 2500 km when fjords are excluded.
Moraine	A moraine is any glacially formed accumulation of unconsolidated glacial debris that occurs in currently glaciated and formerly glaciated regions on Earth (i.e. a past glacial maximum), through geomorphological processes. Moraines are formed from debris previously carried along by a glacier and normally consist of somewhat rounded particles ranging in size from large boulders to minute glacial flour. Lateral moraines are formed at the side of the ice flow and terminal moraines at the foot, marking the maximum advance of the glacier.
Tarim Basin	The Tarim Basin is a large endorheic basin in northwest China occupying an area of about 906,500 km^2 . Located in China's Xinjiang region, it is sometimes used metonymously for the southern half of the province, or Nanjiang (Turkish: tarim havzasi, Chinese: ??; pinyin: Nánjiang; literally 'Southern Xinjiang'). Its northern boundary is the Tian Shan mountain range and its southern boundary is the Kunlun Mountains on the edge of the Qinghai-Tibet Plateau.
Remote sensing	Remote sensing is the acquisition of information about an object or phenomenon without making physical contact with the object. In modern usage, the term generally refers to the use of aerial sensor technologies to detect and classify objects on Earth (both on the surface, and in the atmosphere and oceans) by means of propagated signals (e.g. electromagnetic radiation). It may be split into active remote sensing, when a signal is first emitted from aircraft or satellites) or passive (e.g. sunlight) when information is merely recorded.
Lake	A lake is a body of relatively still water of considerable size, localized in a basin, that is surrounded by land apart from a river, stream, or other form of moving water that serves to feed or drain the lake. Lakes are inland and not part of the ocean and therefore are distinct from lagoons, and are larger and deeper than ponds. Lakes can be contrasted with rivers or streams, which are usually flowing.
Esker	An esker, eskar, eschar, or os, sometimes called an asar, osar, or serpent kame, is a long, winding ridge of stratified sand and gravel, examples of which occur in glaciated and formerly glaciated regions of Europe and North America. Eskers are frequently several kilometres long and, because of their peculiar uniform shape, are somewhat like railway embankments.

18. Glacial and Periglacial Landforms

CHAPTER HIGHLIGHTS & NOTES: KEY TERMS, PEOPLE, PLACES, CONCEPTS

Till plain

A till plain is an extensive flat plain of glacial till that forms when a sheet of ice becomes detached from the main body of a glacier and melts in place, depositing the sediments it carried. Ground moraines are formed when the till melts out of the glacier in irregular heaps, forming rolling hills.

Till plains created by the Wisconsin glaciation cover much of northern Ohio).

Alpine permafrost

In geology, permafrost is ground, including rock or soil, at or below the freezing point of water 0 °C (32 °F) for two or more years. Most permafrost is located in high latitudes (in and around the Arctic and Antarctic regions), but alpine permafrost may exist at high altitudes in much lower latitudes. Ground ice is not always present, as may be in the case of nonporous bedrock, but it frequently occurs and it may be in amounts exceeding the potential hydraulic saturation of the ground material.

Permafrost

In geology, permafrost or cryotic soil is soil at or below the freezing point of water 0 °C for two or more years. Most permafrost is located in high latitudes (i.e. land close to the North and South poles), but alpine permafrost may exist at high altitudes in much lower latitudes. Ground ice is not always present, as may be in the case of nonporous bedrock, but it frequently occurs and it may be in amounts exceeding the potential hydraulic saturation of the ground material.

Pluvial

In geology and climatology, a pluvial was an extended period of abundant rainfall lasting many thousands of years. Pluvial is also applied to the sediments of these periods (e.g. Lake Bonneville, Lake Lahontan, Lake Manly). The term is especially applied to such periods during the Pleistocene Epoch.

Active layer

In environments containing permafrost, the active layer is the top layer of soil that thaws during the summer and freezes again during the autumn. In all climates, whether they contain permafrost or not, the temperature in the lower levels of the soil will remain more stable than that at the surface, where the influence of the ambient temperature is greatest. This means that, over many years, the influence of cooling in winter and heating in summer (in temperate climates) will decrease as depth increases.

Island

An island or isle is any piece of sub-continental land that is surrounded by water. Very small islands such as emergent land features on atolls can be called islets, skerries, cays or keys. An island in a river or a lake island may be called an eyot or ait, or a holm.

Gelifluction

Gelifluction, very similar to solifluction, is the seasonal freeze-thaw action upon waterlogging topsoils which induces downslope movement. Gelifluction is prominent in periglacial regions where snow falls during six to eight months of the year. In spring, the snow and ice melt, and the landscape is effectively inundated with half a year's worth of rainfall in the space of a couple of days.

Patterned ground	Patterned ground is the distinct, and often symmetrical geometric shapes formed by ground material in periglacial regions. Typically found in remote regions of the Arctic, Antarctica, and the Australian outback, but also found anywhere that freezing and thawing of soil alternate; patterned ground has also been observed on Mars. The geometric shapes and patterns associated with patterned ground are often mistaken as artistic human creations.
Thermokarst	Thermokarst is a land surface characterised by very irregular surfaces of marshy hollows and small hummocks formed as ice-rich permafrost thaws, that occurs in Arctic areas, and on a smaller scale in mountainous areas such as the Himalayas and the Swiss Alps. These pitted surfaces resemble those formed by solution in some karst areas of limestone, which is how they came to have karst attached to their name without the presence of any limestone. Small domes that form on the surface due to frost heaving with the onset of winter are only temporary features.
Periglacial	Periglaciation (adjective: 'periglacial,' also referring to places at the edges of glacial areas) describes geomorphic processes that result from seasonal thawing of snow in areas of permafrost, the runoff from which refreezes in ice wedges and other structures. Tundra is a common ecological community in periglacial areas.
SPRING	SPRING is a freeware GIS and remote sensing image processing system with an object-oriented data model which provides for the integration of raster and vector data representations in a single environment. It has Windows and Linux versions and provides a comprehensive set of functions, including tools for Satellite Image Processing, Digital Terrain Modeling, Spatial Analysis, Geostatistics, Spatial Statistics, Spatial Databases and Map Management. SPRING is a product of Brazilian National Institute for Space Research (INPE), who is developing SPRING since 1992, and has required over 200 man/years of development and includes extensive documentation, tutorials and examples.
Deep ocean	The deep sea or deep layer is the lowest layer in the ocean, existing below the thermocline and above the seabed, at a depth of 1000 fathoms or more. Little or no light penetrates this part of the ocean, and most of the organisms that live there rely for subsistence on falling organic matter produced in the photic zone. For this reason, scientists once assumed that life would be sparse in the deep ocean, but virtually every probe has revealed that, on the contrary, life is abundant in the deep ocean.
Ice age	An ice age, or more precisely, a glacial age, is a period of long-term reduction in the temperature of the Earth's surface and atmosphere, resulting in the presence or expansion of continental and polar ice sheets and alpine glaciers. Within a long-term ice age, individual pulses of cold climate are termed 'glacial periods' (or alternatively 'glacials' or 'glaciations' or colloquially as 'ice age'), and intermittent warm periods are called 'interglacials'. Glaciologically, ice age implies the presence of extensive ice sheets in the northern and southern hemispheres.

18. Glacial and Periglacial Landforms

CHAPTER HIGHLIGHTS & NOTES: KEY TERMS, PEOPLE, PLACES, CONCEPTS

Ocean current	An ocean current is a continuous, directed movement of seawater generated by the forces acting upon this mean flow, such as breaking waves, wind, Coriolis effect, cabbeling, temperature and salinity differences and tides caused by the gravitational pull of the Moon and the Sun. Depth contours, shoreline configurations and interaction with other currents influence a current's direction and strength. A deep current is any ocean current at a depth of greater than 100m.
Weathering	Weathering is the breaking down of rocks, soil and minerals as well as artificial materials through contact with the Earth's atmosphere, biota and waters. Weathering occurs in situ, roughly translated to: 'with no movement', and thus should not be confused with erosion, which involves the movement of rocks and minerals by agents such as water, ice, snow, wind, waves and gravity and then being transported and deposited in other locations. Two important classifications of weathering processes exist - physical and chemical weathering; each sometimes involves a biological component.
Current	A current, in a river or stream, is the flow of water influenced by gravity as the water moves downhill to reduce its potential energy. The current varies spatially as well as temporally within the stream, dependent upon the flow volume of water, stream gradient, and channel geometrics. In tidal zones, the current in rivers and streams may reverse on the flood tide before resuming on the ebb tide.
Trough	A 'trough' is an elongated region of relatively low atmospheric pressure, often associated with fronts. Unlike fronts, there is not a universal symbol for a trough on a weather chart. The weather charts in some countries or regions mark troughs by a line.
Insolation	Insolation is a measure of solar radiation energy received on a given surface area and recorded during a given time. It is also called solar irradiation and expressed as 'hourly irradiation' if recorded during an hour or 'daily irradiation' if recorded during a day. The unit recommended by the World Meteorological Organization is megajoules per square metre (MJ/m^2) or joules per square millimetre (J/mm^2).
Siberia	Siberia is an extensive geographical region, consisting of almost all of North Asia. Siberia has been part of Russia since the seventeenth century. The territory of Siberia extends eastwards from the Ural Mountains to the watershed between the Pacific and Arctic drainage basins.

18. Glacial and Periglacial Landforms

CHAPTER QUIZ: KEY TERMS, PEOPLE, PLACES, CONCEPTS

1. A _________ is a theatre-like valley formed by glacial erosion. Alternative names for this landform are corrie (from Scottish Gaelic coire meaning a pot or cauldron) and cwm (Welsh for 'valley', pronounced coom). A _________ may also be a similarly shaped landform arising from fluvial erosion.

   a. New Lanark
   b. Seafloor spreading
   c. Cirque
   d. littoral

2. An _________ is an area less than 50,000 km^2 (19,000 sq mi) of ice often found in the colder climates and higher altitudes of the world where there is sufficient precipitation. It is an extensive area of interconnected valley glaciers from which the higher peaks rise as nunataks. _________s are larger than alpine glaciers, smaller than ice sheets and similar in area to ice caps.

   a. Essay on the Principle of Population
   b. Seafloor spreading
   c. Ice field
   d. littoral

3. Geologically, a fjord or _________ is a long, narrow inlet with steep sides or cliffs, created by glacial erosion. There are many fjords on the coasts of Alaska, British Columbia, Chile, Greenland, Iceland, the Kerguelen Islands, New Zealand, Norway, Labrador, Nunavut, Newfoundland, and Washington state. Norway's coastline is estimated at 29,000 km with fjords, but only 2500 km when fjords are excluded.

   a. Fiord
   b. Biometeorology
   c. Clear-air turbulence
   d. Teniente Luis Carvajal Villaroel Antarctic Base

4. A _________ is a park in use for conservation purposes. Often it is a reserve of natural, semi-natural, or developed land that a sovereign state declares or owns. Although individual nations designate their own _________s differently, there is a common idea: the conservation of 'wild nature' for posterity and as a symbol of national pride.

   a. Mughal Empire
   b. Seafloor spreading
   c. National Park
   d. littoral

5. . In geology and climatology, a _________ was an extended period of abundant rainfall lasting many thousands of years. _________ is also applied to the sediments of these periods (e.g. Lake Bonneville, Lake Lahontan, Lake Manly). The term is especially applied to such periods during the Pleistocene Epoch.

   a. 8.2 kiloyear event
   b. Bi-hemispherical reflectance
   c. Pluvial

ANSWER KEY
18. Glacial and Periglacial Landforms

---

1. c
2. c
3. a
4. c
5. c

Other Facts101 e-Books and Tests

CPSIA information can be obtained
at www.ICGtesting.com
Printed in the USA
FSHW021606231219
65393FS

9 781538 832844